O9-AHU-609

To

_____

From

_____

Date

_____

God's Priorities
FOR YOUR LIFE

FOR TEENS

HENDRICKSON
PUBLISHERS

God's Priorities for Your Life for Teens

©2006 Hendrickson Publishers, Inc.
P. O. Box 3473
Peabody, MA 01961

ISBN-13: 978-1-59856-134-0
ISBN-10: 1-59856-134-0

All rights reserved. Except for brief quotations used in reviews, articles, or other media, no part of this book may be reproduced or transmitted in any form or by any means, electronic or mechanical, including photocopying, recording, or by information storage or retrieval system, without permission by the publisher.

Printed in the United States of America

First printing—August 2006

Except for quotations from Scripture, the quoted ideas expressed in this book are not, in all cases, exact quotations, as some have been edited for clarity and brevity. In all cases, the author has attempted to maintain the speaker's original intent. In some cases, quoted material for this book was obtained from secondary sources, primarily print media. While every effort was made to ensure the accuracy of these sources, the accuracy cannot be guaranteed. For additions, deletions, corrections, or clarifications in future editions of this text, please write Hendrickson Publishers, Inc.

Scriptures marked NIV® are from the Holy Bible, New International Version®. Copyright © 1973, 1978, 1984 by International Bible Society. Used by permission of Zondervan Publishing House. All rights reserved.

Scriptures marked NASB are taken from the New American Standard Bible®. © Copyright The Lockman Foundation 1960, 1962, 1963, 1968, 1971, 1972, 1973, 1975, 1977, 1995. Used by permission. (www.Lockman.org).

Scriptures marked NKJV are taken from the New King James Version®. Copyright © 1982 by Thomas Nelson, Inc. Used by permission. All rights reserved.

Scriptures marked NLT are taken from the Holy Bible, New Living Translation, copyright © 1996. Used by permission of Tyndale House Publishers, Inc., Wheaton, Illinois 60189. All rights reserved.

Scriptures marked NCV are quoted from The Holy Bible, New Century Version, copyright © 1987, 1988, 1991 by Word Publishing, Nashville, Tennessee 37214. Used by permission.

Scriptures marked KJV are taken from the King James Version.

Scripture quotations marked MSG are taken from The Message. Copyright © by Eugene H. Peterson 1993, 1994, 1995. Used by permission of NavPress Publishing Group.

Scripture quotations marked ICB are taken from the International Children's Bible, New Century Version © 1986, 1988 by Word Publishing, Nashville, Tennessee 37214. Used by permission.

Scripture quotations marked TLB are taken from The Living Bible copyright © 1971. Used by permission of Tyndale House Publishers, Inc., Wheaton, Illinois 60189. All rights reserved.

Scripture quotations marked Holman CSB are taken from the Holman Christian Standard Bible®, Copyright © 1999, 2000, 2002, 2003 by Holman Bible Publishers. Used by permission. Holman Christian Standard Bible®, Holman CSB®, and HCSB® are federally registered trademarks of Holman Bible Publishers.

Cover Design by Kim Russell / Wahoo Designs
Page Layout by Bart Dawson

God's Priorities
FOR YOUR LIFE

FOR TEENS

Table of Contents

Introduction

How many decisions do you make in a typical day? When you stop to think about it, you make thousands of choices, usually without too much forethought. Of course, most of these choices are relatively small ones, like what to do at a given moment, or what to say, or how to direct your thoughts. And make no mistake: your choices are shaped by your priorities. Simply put, your priorities determine, to a surprising extent, the quality of the decisions you make and the direction that your life will take. And that's why the ideas in this book are so important.

This book addresses Christian values that can—and should—shape your life. You may find it helpful to read the book from cover to cover, or you may decide to scan the Table of Contents and then turn to the chapters that seem particularly important to you. Either way, the ideas on these pages will serve to remind you of God's commandments, God's promises, God's love, and God's Son—all things that are crucially important as you establish priorities for the next stage of your life's journey.

Whose values do you hold most dear: society's values or God's values? When you decide to make God's priorities your priorities, you will receive His abundance and His peace. When you make God a full partner in every aspect of your life, He will lead you along the proper path: His path. When you allow God to direct your steps, He will honor you with spiritual blessings that are simply too numerous to count. So, as you make your next important decision, pause to consider the values that serve as the starting point for that decision. When you do, your decision-making will be vastly improved . . . and so will your life.

A life touched by God always ends in touching others.

Erwin McManus

*Let us fix our eyes on Jesus, the author
and perfecter of our faith, who for the joy
set before him endured the cross,
scorning its shame, and sat down
at the right hand of the throne of God.*

Hebrews 12:2 NIV

Priorities for Life

First pay attention to me, and then relax.
Now you can take it easy—you're in good hands.

Proverbs 1:33 MSG

Sure you're a busy person, and sure you've lots of things to do, but remember this: everything on your to-do list is not created equal. Certain tasks are extremely important while others are not. Therefore, it's important that prioritize your daily activities and complete each task in the approximate order of its importance.

The principle of doing first things first is simple in theory but more complicated in practice. Well-meaning family, friends, and coworkers have a way of making unexpected demands upon your time. Furthermore, each day has its own share of minor emergencies; these urgent matters tend to draw your attention away from more important ones. On paper, prioritizing is simple, but to act upon those priorities in the real world requires maturity, patience, determination, and balance.

If you fail to prioritize your day, life will automatically do the job for you. So your choice is simple: prioritize or be prioritized. It's a choice that will help determine the quality of your life.

Are you living a balanced life that allows time for worship, for family, for school, for exercise, and a little time left over for you? Or do you feel overworked, under-appreciated, and overwhelmed? If your to-do list is "maxed out" and your energy is on the wane, it's time to restore a sense of balance to your life. You can do so by turning the concerns and the priorities of this day over to God—prayerfully, earnestly, and often. Then, you must listen for His answer . . . and trust the answer He gives.

Great relief and satisfaction can come from seeking
God's priorities for us in each season, discerning what
is "best" in the midst of many noble opportunities,
and pouring our most excellent energies into those things.

Beth Moore

PRIORITIES FOR MY LIFE

Make time for God. Even if your day is filled to the brim with obligations and priorities, no priority is greater than our obligation to our Creator. Make sure to give Him the time He deserves, not only on Sundays, but also on every other day of the week.

TIMELESS WISDOM FOR GODLY LIVING

Setting goals is one way you can be sure that you will focus your efforts on the main things so that trivial matters will not become your focus.

Charles Stanley

Give me the person who says, "This one thing I do, and not these fifty things I dabble in."

D. L. Moody

One hundred years from now it won't matter if you got that big break, or finally traded up to a Mercedes. It will greatly matter, one hundred years from now, that you made a commitment to Jesus Christ.

David Shibley

And I pray this: that your love will keep on growing in knowledge and every kind of discernment, so that you can determine what really matters and can be pure and blameless in the day of Christ.

Philippians 1:9 Holman CSB

Often our lives are strangled by things that don't ultimately matter.

Grady Nutt

MORE WORDS FROM GOD'S WORD

The thing you should want most is God's kingdom and doing what God wants. Then all these other things you need will be given to you.

Matthew 6:33 NCV

He said to them all, "If anyone desires to come after Me, let him deny himself, and take up his cross daily, and follow Me. For whoever desires to save his life will lose it, but whoever loses his life for My sake will save it."

Luke 9:23-24 NKJV

In a race, everyone runs but only one person gets first prize . . . to win the contest you must deny yourselves many things that would keep you from doing your best.

1 Corinthians 9:24-25 TLB

My Priorities for Life

I understand the importance of reviewing my priorities frequently.

On my priority list, I put God first.

I place a high value on doing important tasks first and easy tasks later.

Check Your Priority		
High	Med.	Low
—	—	—
—	—	—
—	—	—

Life with a Capital L

*Make it your ambition to lead a quiet life, to mind your own business
and to work with your hands, just as we told you, so that your
daily life may win the respect of outsiders and so that
you will not be dependent on anybody.*

1 Thessalonians 4:11-12 NIV

Life can be tough sometimes, but it's also wonderful—and it's a glorious gift from God. How will you use that gift? Will you treat this day as a precious treasure from your Heavenly Father, or will you take the next 24 hours for granted? The answer should be obvious: Every day, including this one, comes gift-wrapped from God—your job is to unwrap that gift, to use it wisely, and to give thanks to the Giver.

Instead of sleepwalking through life, you must wake up and live in the precious present. Each waking moment holds the potential to celebrate, to serve, to share, or to love. Because you are a person with incalculable potential, each moment has incalculable value. Your challenge is to experience each day to the fullest as you seek to live in accordance with God's plan for your life. When you do, you'll experience His abundance and His peace.

Are you willing to treat this day (and every one hereafter) as a special gift to be savored and celebrated? You should—and if you seek to Live with a capital L, you most certainly will.

In pretending, there is safety, a middle-of-the-road,
stick-with-the-flavor-you-know kind of living.
But I believe that God meant for life to take our breath away,
sometimes because of the sheer joy of it all and sometimes
because of the severe pain. To choose living over
pretending means that we will know both.

Angela Thomas

PRIORITIES FOR MY LIFE

Be a realistic optimist about life, and remember that your attitude toward the future will help create your future. You might as well put the self-fulfilling prophecy to work for you, and besides, life is far too short to be a pessimist.

TIMELESS WISDOM FOR GODLY LIVING

The Bible says that being a Christian is not only a great way to die, but it's also the best way to live.

Bill Hybels

Whether we preach, pray, write, do business, travel, take care of children, or administer the government—whatever we do—our whole life and influence should be filled with the power of the Holy Spirit.

Charles Finney

You've heard the saying, "Life is what you make it." That means we have a choice. We can choose to have a life full of frustration and fear, but we can just as easily choose one of joy and contentment.

Dennis Swanberg

I came so they can have real and eternal life, more and better life than they ever dreamed of.
John 10:10 MSG

Wherever you are, be all there. Live to the hilt every situation you believe to be the will of God.

Jim Elliot

MORE WORDS FROM GOD'S WORD

I am the way and the truth and the life. No one comes to the Father except through me.

John 14:6 NIV

Watch your life and doctrine closely. Persevere in them, because if you do, you will save both yourself and your hearers.

1 Timothy 4:16 NIV

His divine power has given us everything we need for life and godliness through our knowledge of him who called us by his own glory and goodness.

2 Peter 1:3 NIV

My Priorities for Life

	Check Your Priority		
	High	Med.	Low

I consider my life to be a priceless gift from God.

— — —

I slow down to marvel at the beauty of God's glorious creation.

— — —

I strive to make this day—and every day—a cause for celebration.

— — —

I understand the importance of spending time each day thanking God for His blessings.

— — —

The Direction of Your Thoughts

And now, dear brothers and sisters, let me say one more thing as I close this letter. Fix your thoughts on what is true and honorable and right. Think about things that are pure and lovely and admirable. Think about things that are excellent and worthy of praise.

Philippians 4:8 NLT

Our thoughts have the power to shape our lives—for better or worse. Thoughts have the power to lift our spirits, to improve our circumstances, and to strengthen our relationship with the Creator. But, our thoughts also have the power to cause us great harm if we focus too intently upon those things that distance us from God.

How will you direct your thoughts today? Will you obey the words of Philippians 4:8 by dwelling upon those things that are honorable, true, and worthy of praise? Or will you allow your thoughts to be hijacked by the negativity that seems to dominate our troubled world?

Are you fearful, angry, bored, or worried? Are you so preoccupied with the concerns of this day that you fail to thank God for the promise of eternity? Are you confused, bitter, or pessimistic? If so, God wants to have a little talk with you.

God intends that you experience joy and abundance, but He will not force His joy upon you; you must claim it for yourself. It's up to you to celebrate the life that God has given you by focusing your mind upon "whatever is of good repute." Today, spend more time thinking about your blessings, and less time fretting about your hardships. Then, take time to thank the Giver of all things good for gifts that are, in truth, far too numerous to count.

Preoccupy my thoughts with your praise beginning today.

Joni Eareckson Tada

PRIORITIES FOR MY LIFE

Good thoughts create good deeds. Good thoughts lead to good deeds and bad thoughts lead elsewhere. So guard your thoughts accordingly.

TIMELESS WISDOM FOR GODLY LIVING

Make yourselves nests of pleasant thoughts.

John Ruskin

People who do not develop and practice good thinking often find themselves at the mercy of their circumstances.

John Maxwell

I am amazed at my own "rut-think" that periodically takes over.

Marilyn Meberg

It is the thoughts and intents of the heart that shape a person's life.

John Eldredge

Come near to God, and God will come near to you.
You sinners, clean sin out of your lives.
You who are trying to follow God and the world
at the same time, make your thinking pure.
James 4:8 NCV

The mind is like a clock that is constantly running down. It has to be wound up daily with good thoughts.

Fulton J. Sheen

MORE WORDS FROM GOD'S WORD

Those who are pure in their thinking are happy, because they will be with God.

Matthew 5:8 NCV

So prepare your minds for service and have self-control.

1 Peter 1:13 NCV

I, the Lord, examine the mind, I test the heart to give to each according to his way, according to what his actions deserve.

Jeremiah 17:10 Holman CSB

Commit your works to the Lord, and your thoughts will be established.

Proverbs 16:3 NKJV

My Priorities for Life

	Check Your Priority		
	High	Med.	Low
I understand the importance of directing my thoughts in a proper direction.	—	—	—
I believe that emotions are contagious, so I try to associate with people who are upbeat, optimistic, and encouraging.	—	—	—
I understand that when I dwell on positive thoughts, I feel better about myself and my circumstances.	—	—	—

The Journey Toward Spiritual Maturity

For this reason we also, since the day we heard it,
do not cease to pray for you, and to ask that you may be
filled with the knowledge of His will in all wisdom
and spiritual understanding.

Colossians 1:9 NKJV

When it comes to your faith, God doesn't intend for you to stand still. He wants you to keep moving and growing. In fact, God's plan for you includes a lifetime of prayer, praise, and spiritual growth.

When we cease to grow, either emotionally or spiritually, we do ourselves and our loved ones a profound disservice. But, if we study God's Word, if we obey His commandments, and if we live in the center of His will, we will not be "stagnant" believers; we will, instead, be growing Christians . . . and that's exactly what God wants for our lives.

Many of life's most important lessons are painful to learn. During times of heartbreak and hardship, we must be courageous and we must be patient, knowing that in His own time, God will heal us if we invite Him into our hearts.

Spiritual growth need not take place only in times of adversity. We must seek to grow in our knowledge and love of the Lord every day that we live. In those quiet moments when we open our hearts to God, the One who made us keeps remaking us. He gives us direction, perspective, wisdom, and courage. The appropriate moment to accept those spiritual gifts is the present one.

Are you as mature as you're ever going to be? Hopefully not! When it comes to your faith, God doesn't intend for you to become "fully grown," at least not in this lifetime. In fact, God still has important lessons that He intends to teach you. So ask yourself this: what lesson is God trying to teach me today? And then go about the business of learning it.

The whole idea of belonging to Christ is to look less and less like we used to and more and more like Him.

Angela Thomas

PRIORITIES FOR MY LIFE

How do I know if I can still keep growing as a Christian? Check your pulse. If it's still beating, then you can still keep growing.

TIMELESS WISDOM FOR GODLY LIVING

Enjoy the adventure of receiving God guidance. Taste it, revel in it, appreciate the fact that the journey is often a lot more exciting than arriving at the destination.

Bill Hybels

Grace meets you where you are, but it doesn't leave you where it found you.

Anne Lamott

Some people have received Christ but have never reached spiritual maturity. We should grow as Christians every day, and we are not completely mature until we live in the presence of Christ.

Billy Graham

> *So let us stop going over the basics of Christianity again and again. Let us go on instead and become mature in our understanding.*
>
> *Hebrews 6:1 NLT*

Recently I've been learning that life comes down to this: God is in everything. Regardless of what difficulties I am experiencing at the moment, or what things aren't as I would like them to be, I look at the circumstances and say, "Lord, what are you trying to teach me?"

Catherine Marshall

MORE WORDS FROM GOD'S WORD

*But grow in the grace and knowledge of our Lord and Savior Jesus Christ.
To Him be the glory both now and to the day of eternity.*

2 Peter 3:18 Holman CSB

*Know the love of Christ which surpasses knowledge, that you may be
filled up to all the fullness of God.*

Ephesians 3:19 NASB

*For You, O God, have tested us; You have refined us as silver is refined.
You brought us into the net; You laid affliction on our backs. You have
caused men to ride over our heads; we went through fire and through
water; but You brought us out to rich fulfillment.*

Psalm 66:10–12 NKJV

My Priorities for Life

I believe that the level of my spiritual maturity has
a direct impact, either positively or negatively,
on those around me.

Since I believe that I still have "room to grow" in
my faith, gaining spiritual maturity remains
a priority for me.

Since I feel that spiritual growth happens day by
day, I will live, worship, and pray accordingly.

Check Your Priority		
High	Med.	Low
—	—	—
—	—	—
—	—	—

Doing
What's Right

In everything set them an example by doing what is good.

Titus 2:7 NIV

If you're like most people, you seek the admiration of your friends and acquaintances. But the eagerness to please others should never overshadow your eagerness to please God. If you seek to fulfill the purposes that God has in store for you, then you must be a "doer of the word." And how can you do so? By putting God first.

The words of Matthew 6:33 make it clear: "But seek first the kingdom of God and His righteousness, and all these things will be provided for you" (Holman CSB). God has given you a priceless guidebook, an indispensable tool for "seeking His kingdom." That tool, of course, is the Holy Bible. It contains thorough instructions which, if followed, lead to fulfillment, righteousness and salvation.

But for those who would ignore God's Word, Martin Luther issued this stern warning: "You may as well quit reading and hearing the Word of God and give it to the devil if you do not desire to live according to it." Luther understood that obedience leads to abundance just as surely as disobedience leads to disaster; you should understand it, too.

Each new day presents countless opportunities to put God in first place . . . or not. When you honor Him by living according to His commandments, you earn the abundance and peace that He promises. But, if you ignore God's teachings, you will inevitably bring needless suffering upon yourself and your family.

Would you like a time-tested formula for successful living? Here it is: Don't just listen to God's Word, live by it. Does this sound too simple? Perhaps it is simple, but it is also the only way to reap the marvelous riches that God has in store for you.

More depends on my walk than my talk.

D. L. Moody

PRIORITIES FOR MY LIFE

Obey God or face the consequences: God rewards obedience and punishes disobedience. It's not enough to understand God's rules; you must also live by them . . . or else.

TIMELESS WISDOM FOR GODLY LIVING

Study the Bible and observe how the persons behaved and how God dealt with them. There is explicit teaching on every condition of life.

Corrie ten Boom

It is by acts and not by ideas that people live.

Harry Emerson Fosdick

What you do reveals what you believe about God, regardless of what you say. When God reveals what He has purposed to do, you face a crisis—a decision time. God and the world can tell from your response what you really believe about God.

Henry Blackaby

Are there those among you who are truly wise and understanding? Then they should show it by living right and doing good things with a gentleness that comes from wisdom.
James 3:13 NCV

Although God causes all things to work together for good for His children, He still holds us accountable for our behavior.

Kay Arthur

MORE WORDS FROM GOD'S WORD

Even a child is known by his actions, by whether his conduct is pure and right.

Proverbs 20:11 NIV

Here is a simple, rule-of-thumb for behavior: Ask yourself what you want people to do for you, then grab the initiative and do it for them. Add up God's Law and Prophets and this is what you get.

Matthew 7:12 MSG

Light shines on the godly, and joy on those who do right. May all who are godly be happy in the Lord and praise his holy name.

Psalm 97:11-12 NLT

He will teach us of his ways, and we will walk in his paths.

Isaiah 2:3 KJV

My Priorities for Life

	Check Your Priority	
	High Med. Low	

I understand that my behavior reveals my relationship with God.

— — —

I understand that my behavior affects how I feel about myself.

— — —

I know that my behavior should reflect Biblical values.

— — —

God Is Perfect; We Are Not

Those who wait for perfect weather will never plant seeds;
those who look at every cloud will never harvest crops.
Plant early in the morning, and work until evening, because
you don't know if this or that will succeed. They might both do well.

Ecclesiastes 11:4, 6 NCV

You live in a world where expectations are high, incredibly high, or unreachable. The media delivers an endless stream of messages that tell you how to look, how to behave, how to eat, and how to dress. The media's expectations are impossible to meet—God's are not. God doesn't expect you to be perfect . . . and neither should you.

If you find yourself bound up by the chains of perfectionism, it's time to ask yourself who you're trying to impress, and why. If you're trying to impress other people, it's time to reconsider your priorities.

Remember this: the expectations that really matter are not society's expectations or your friends' expectations. The expectations that matter are God's expectations, pure and simple. And everything else should take a back seat.

So do your best to please God, and don't worry too much about what other people think. And, when it comes to meeting the unrealistic expectations of our crazy world, forget about trying to meet those unrealistic expectations and concentrate, instead, on living a life that's pleasing to God.

God has the marvelous ability
to love us in the midst
of our imperfections.

Joyce Meyer

PRIORITIES FOR MY LIFE

Accept your own imperfections! If you're caught up in the modern-day push toward perfection, grow up . . . and then lighten up on yourself.

TIMELESS WISDOM FOR GODLY LIVING

A good garden may have some weeds.

Thomas Fuller

What makes a Christian a Christian is not perfection but forgiveness.

Max Lucado

Nothing would be done at all, if a man waited until he could do it so well that no one could find fault with it.

John Henry Cardinal Newman

The happiest people in the world are not those who have no problems, but the people who have learned to live with those things that are less than perfect.

James Dobson

Your beliefs about these things should be kept secret between you and God. People are happy if they can do what they think is right without feeling guilty.

Romans 14:22 NCV

Excellence is not perfection, but essentially a desire to be strong in the Lord and for the Lord.

Cynthia Heald

MORE WORDS FROM GOD'S WORD

The fear of human opinion disables; trusting in God protects you from that.

Proverbs 29:25 MSG

In thee, O Lord, do I put my trust; let me never be put into confusion.

Psalm 71:1 KJV

Teach me Your way, O LORD; I will walk in Your truth.

Psalm 86:11 NASB

Let us lay aside every weight and the sin that so easily ensnares us, and run with endurance the race that lies before us, keeping our eyes on Jesus, the source and perfecter of our faith.

Hebrews 12:1-2 Holman CSB

My Priorities for Life

I am willing to accept the inevitable imperfections in others.

I am willing to do my best, and leave the results up to God.

I think that it is important to acknowledge the difference between perfectionism and excellence.

Check Your Priority		
High	Med.	Low
—	—	—
—	—	—
—	—	—

Opportunities Everywhere

Therefore, as we have opportunity, we must work for the good of all,
especially for those who belong to the household of faith.

Galatians 6:10 Holman CSB

As you look at the landscape of your life, do you see opportunities, possibilities, and blessings, or do you focus, instead, upon the more negative scenery? Do you spend more time counting your blessings or your misfortunes? If you've acquired the unfortunate habit of focusing too intently upon the negative aspects of life, then your spiritual vision is in need of correction.

Whether you realize it or not, opportunities are whirling around you like stars crossing the night sky: beautiful to observe, but too numerous to count. Yet you may be too concerned with the challenges of everyday living to notice those opportunities. That's why you should slow down occasionally, catch your breath, and focus your thoughts on two things: the talents God has given you and the opportunities that He has placed before you. God is leading you in the direction of those opportunities. Your task is to watch carefully, to pray fervently, and to act accordingly.

Are you willing to place your future in the hands of a loving and all-knowing God? Do you trust in the ultimate goodness of His plan for your life? Will you face today's challenges with optimism and hope? You should. After all, God created you for a very important purpose: His purpose. And you still have important work to do: His work. And the time to start doing that work is now.

Worry is the senseless process of cluttering up tomorrow's opportunities with leftover problems from today.

Barbara Johnson

PRIORITIES FOR MY LIFE

Familiarize yourself with the opportunities of tomorrow. Tomorrow is filled with opportunities for people who are willing to find them and work for them. Make certain that you have more than a passing familiarity with the ever-shifting sands of our changing world.

TIMELESS WISDOM FOR GODLY LIVING

Life is a glorious opportunity.

Billy Graham

Every day we live is a priceless gift of God, loaded with possibilities to learn something new, to gain fresh insights.

Dale Evans Rogers

God specializes in things fresh and firsthand. His plans for you this year may outshine those of the past. He's prepared to fill your days with reasons to give Him praise.

Joni Eareckson Tada

Great opportunities often disguise themselves in small tasks.

Rick Warren

Make the most of every opportunity.
Colossians 4:5 NIV

God surrounds you with opportunity. You and I are free in Jesus Christ, not to do whatever we want, but to be all that God wants us to be.

Warren Wiersbe

MORE WORDS FROM GOD'S WORD

Let us not lose heart in doing good, for in due time we shall reap if we do not grow weary. So then, while we have opportunity, let us do good to all men, and especially to those who are of the household of the faith.

Galatians 6:9-10 NASB

Dear brothers and sisters, whenever trouble comes your way, let it be an opportunity for joy. For when your faith is tested, your endurance has a chance to grow. So let it grow, for when your endurance is fully developed, you will be strong in character and ready for anything.

James 1:2-4 NLT

Remember ye not the former things, neither consider the things of old. Behold, I will do a new thing . . . .

Isaiah 43:18-19 KJV

My Priorities for Life

	Check Your Priority		
	High	Med.	Low
I understand that life is brief, and I will strive to make the most of my time here on earth.	—	—	—
I understand the importance of looking for opportunities, not stumbling blocks.	—	—	—
I trust that God has important things for me to do.	—	—	—

Living on Purpose

Whatever you do, do all to the glory of God.

1 Corinthians 10:31 NKJV

L ife is best lived on purpose, not by accident: the sooner we discover what God intends for us to do with our lives, the better. But God's purposes aren't always clear to us. Sometimes we wander aimlessly in a wilderness of our own making. And sometimes, we struggle mightily against God in a vain effort to find success and happiness through our own means, not His.

Whenever we struggle against God's plans, we suffer. When we resist God's calling, our efforts bear little fruit. Our best strategy, therefore, is to seek God's wisdom and to follow Him wherever He chooses to lead. When we do so, we are blessed.

When we align ourselves with God's purposes, we avail ourselves of His power and His peace. But how can we know precisely what God's intentions are? The answer, of course, is that even the most well-intentioned believers face periods of uncertainty and doubt about the direction of their lives. So, too, will you.

When you arrive at one of life's inevitable crossroads, that is precisely the moment when you should turn your thoughts and prayers toward God. When you do, He will make Himself known to you in a time and manner of His choosing.

Are you earnestly seeking to discern God's purpose for your life? If so, remember this: 1. God has a plan for your life; 2. If you seek that plan sincerely and prayerfully, you will find it; 3. When you discover God's purpose for your life, you will experience abundance, peace, joy, and power—God's power. And that's the only kind of power that really matters.

Yesterday is just experience but tomorrow is glistening with purpose—and today is the channel leading from one to the other.

Barbara Johnson

We know that all things work together for the good of those who love God: those who are called according to His purpose.

Romans 8:28 Holman CSB

PRIORITIES FOR MY LIFE

Discovering God's purpose for your life requires a willingness to be open. God's plan is unfolding day by day. If you keep your eyes and your heart open, He'll reveal His plans. God has big things in store for you, but He may have quite a few lessons to teach you before you are fully prepared to do His will and fulfill His purposes.

TIMELESS WISDOM FOR GODLY LIVING

Only God's chosen task for you will ultimately satisfy. Do not wait until it is too late to realize the privilege of serving Him in His chosen position for you.

Beth Moore

It's incredible to realize that what we do each day has meaning in the big picture of God's plan.

Bill Hybels

Aim at Heaven and you will get earth "thrown in"; aim at earth and you will get neither.

C. S. Lewis

Until your purpose lines up with God's purpose, you will never be happy or fulfilled.

Charles Stanley

You're sons of Light, daughters of Day.
We live under wide open skies and know where we stand.
So let's not sleepwalk through life . . .
1 Thessalonians 5:5-6 MSG

We aren't just thrown on this earth like dice tossed across a table. We are lovingly placed here for a purpose.

Charles Swindoll

MORE WORDS FROM GOD'S WORD

We look at this Son and see the God who cannot be seen. We look at this Son and see God's original purpose in everything created.

Colossians 1:15 MSG

To everything there is a season, a time for every purpose under heaven.

Ecclesiastes 3:1 NKJV

There is one thing I always do. Forgetting the past and straining toward what is ahead, I keep trying to reach the goal and get the prize for which God called me . . . .

Philippians 3:13–14 NCV

My Priorities for Life

	Check Your Priority		
	High	Med.	Low
I understand the importance of discovering God's unfolding purpose for my life.	—	—	—
I consult God on matters great and small.	—	—	—
I pray about my plans for the future.	—	—	—
I remain open to the opportunities and challenges that God places before me.	—	—	—

Good Samaritan 101

When we have the opportunity to help anyone, we should do it.
But we should give special attention to those who are
in the family of believers.

Galatians 6:10 NCV

Sometimes we would like to help make the world a better place, but we're not sure of the best way to do it. Jesus told the story of the "Good Samaritan," a man who helped a fellow traveler when no one else would. We, too, should be good Samaritans when we encounter people who need our help.

The words of Jesus are unambiguous: "Freely you have received, freely give" (Matthew 10:8 NIV). As followers of Christ, we are commanded to be generous with our friends, with our families, and with those in need. We must give freely of our time, our possessions, and, most especially, our love.

In 2 Corinthians 9, Paul reminds us that when we sow the seeds of generosity, we reap bountiful rewards in accordance with God's plan for our lives: "Now this I say, he who sows sparingly will also reap sparingly, and he who sows bountifully will also reap bountifully. Each one must do just as he has purposed in his heart, not grudgingly or under compulsion, for God loves a cheerful giver" (vv. 6, 7 KJV).

Today, take God's words to heart and make this pledge: Wherever you happen to be, be a good Samaritan. Somebody near you needs your assistance, and you need the spiritual rewards that will be yours when you lend a helping hand.

The truest help we can render an afflicted man is not to take his burden from him, but to call out his best energy, that he may be able to bear the burden himself.

Phillips Brooks

No one stands taller in the climb to success than when he bends over to help up someone else.

John Maxwell

PRIORITIES FOR MY LIFE

Someone very near you may need a helping hand or a kind word, so keep your eyes open, and look for people who need your help, whether at home, at church, or at school.

TIMELESS WISDOM FOR GODLY LIVING

I never look at the masses as my responsibility. I look at the individual. I can love only one person at a time. I can feed only one person at a time. Just one, one, one. You get closer to Christ by coming closer to each other.

Mother Teresa

Do all the good you can. By all the means you can. In all the ways you can. In all the places you can. At all the times you can. To all the people you can. As long as ever you can.

John Wesley

Make it a rule, and pray to God to help you to keep it, never, if possible, to lie down at night without being able to say: "I have made one human being at least a little wiser, or a little happier, or at least a little better this day."

Charles Kingsley

Whenever you are able, do good to people who need help.
Proverbs 3:27 NCV

No matter how crazy or nutty your life has seemed, God can make something strong and good out of it. He can help you grow wide branches for others to use as shelter.

Barbara Johnson

MORE WORDS FROM GOD'S WORD

Then a Samaritan traveling down the road came to where the hurt man was. When he saw the man, he felt very sorry for him. The Samaritan went to him, poured olive oil and wine on his wounds, and bandaged them. Then he put the hurt man on his own donkey and took him to an inn where he cared for him.

Luke 10:33-34 NCV

Carry one another's burdens; in this way you will fulfill the law of Christ.

Galatians 6:2 Holman CSB

I tell you the truth, whatever you did for one of the least of these brothers of mine, you did for me.

Matthew 25:40 NIV

My Priorities for Life

I believe God wants me to help others.

I understand that whenever I help other people, I feel better about myself.

I look for creative ways to lend a helping hand whenever I can.

Check Your Priority		
High	Med.	Low
—	—	—
—	—	—
—	—	—

He Is Here

Come near to God, and God will come near to you.
You sinners, clean sin out of your lives. You who are trying to
follow God and the world at the same time, make your thinking pure.

James 4:8 NCV

Do you ever wonder if God really hears your prayers? If so, you're in good company: lots of very faithful Christians have wondered the same thing. In fact, some of the biggest heroes in the Bible had their doubts—and so, perhaps, will you. But when you have your doubts, remember this: God isn't on vacation, and He hasn't moved out of town. God isn't taking a coffee break, and He isn't snoozing on the couch. He's right here, right now, listening to your thoughts and prayers, watching over your every move.

Do you schedule a regular meeting each day with your Creator? You should. During these moments of stillness, you will gain direction, perspective, and peace—God's peace.

The comforting words of Psalm 46:10 remind us to "Be still, and know that I am God." When we do so, we sense the loving presence of our Heavenly Father, and we are comforted by the certain knowledge that God is not far away . . . and He isn't even nearby. He is, quite literally, here. And it's up to each of us to sense His presence.

Sometimes, you will allow yourself to become very busy, and that's when you may be tempted to ignore God. But, when you quiet yourself long enough to acknowledge His presence, God will touch your heart and restore your spirits. By the way, He's ready to talk right now. Are you?

What a comfort to know that God is present there in your life,
available to meet every situation with you,
that you are never left to face any problem alone.

Vonette Bright

PRIORITIES FOR MY LIFE

Having trouble hearing God? If so, slow yourself down, tune out the distractions, and listen carefully. God has important things to say; your task is to be still and listen.

TIMELESS WISDOM FOR GODLY LIVING

I think we Christians have become lazy. We would rather read a book about how someone else became closer to God than spend time alone with him ourselves.

Sheila Walsh

God is sort of like the wind in that we see evidence of his presence; yet he isn't easily grasped.

Patsy Clairmont

I have a capacity in my soul for taking in God entirely. I am as sure as I live that nothing is so near to me as God. God is nearer to me than I am to myself; my existence depends on the nearness and the presence of God.

Meister Eckhart

> *No, I will not abandon you as orphans—*
> *I will come to you.*
> John 14:18 NLT

When we are in the presence of God, removed from distractions, we are able to hear him more clearly, and a secure environment has been established for the young and broken places in our hearts to surface.

John Eldredge

MORE WORDS FROM GOD'S WORD

For the eyes of the Lord range throughout the earth to strengthen those whose hearts are fully committed to him.

2 Chronicles 16:9 NIV

God did this so that men would seek him and perhaps reach out for him and find him, though he is not far from each one of us.

Acts 17:27 NIV

Surely goodness and mercy shall follow me all the days of my life: and I will dwell in the house of the Lord for ever.

Psalm 23:6 KJV

I am not alone, because the Father is with Me.

John 16:32 Holman CSB

My Priorities for Life

	Check Your Priority		
	High	Med.	Low
I place value upon quiet communication with God.	—	—	—
I am comforted by God's presence, and I seek Him often.	—	—	—
I believe it is important to have a regular time of prayer and reflection.	—	—	—

Be a
Cheerful Giver

God has given gifts to each of you from his great variety of spiritual gifts.
Manage them well so that God's generosity can flow through you.

1 Peter 4:10 NLT

Your blessings from God are too numerous to count.
Those blessings include life, family, friends, talents, and
possessions, for starters. But, your greatest blessing—a gift
that is yours for the asking—is God's gift of salvation through
Christ Jesus. Today, give thanks for your blessings and show your
thanks by using them and by sharing them.

The thread of generosity is woven—completely and
inextricably—into the very fabric of Christ's teachings. He
reminded His followers that, "Whatever you did for one of the
least of these brothers of mine, you did for me" (Matthew 25:40
NIV). The implication is clear: If we genuinely seek to follow
Christ, we must share our time, our possessions, our love, and
our faith.

Today, as you go about the business of living your life, be
more generous than necessary. This world needs every bit of
kindness and generosity that springs from the hearts of believers
like you. Your generosity will glorify the One who has been so
generous to you, and your kindness will touch the hearts of

friends and strangers alike. And, be assured that no good deed is ever wasted. Every time that you share a kind word or a generous gift with another human being, you have also shared it with the Savior of the world.

All the blessings we enjoy are divine deposits,
committed to our trust on this condition:
that they should be dispensed for
the benefit of our neighbors.

John Calvin

PRIORITIES FOR MY LIFE

There is a direct relationship between generosity and joy—the more you give to others, the more joy you will experience for yourself.

TIMELESS WISDOM FOR GODLY LIVING

Anything done for another is done for oneself.

Pope John Paul II

To show great love for God and our neighbor, we need not do great things. It is how much love we put in the doing that makes our offering something beautiful for God.

Mother Teresa

I don't know of anything that will take your eyes off your own situation faster than giving to others.

Mary Hunt

God does not supply money to satisfy our every whim and desire. His promise is to meet our needs and provide an abundance so that we can help other people.

Larry Burkett

The good person is generous and lends lavishly . . . .
Psalm 112:5 MSG

The mark of a Christian is that he will walk the second mile and turn the other cheek. A wise man or woman gives the extra effort, all for the glory of the Lord Jesus Christ.

John Maxwell

MORE WORDS FROM GOD'S WORD

In every way I've shown you that by laboring like this, it is necessary to help the weak and to keep in mind the words of the Lord Jesus, for He said, "It is more blessed to give than to receive."

Acts 20:35 Holman CSB

Be generous: Invest in acts of charity. Charity yields high returns.

Ecclesiastes 11:1 MSG

Whenever we have the opportunity, we should do good to everyone, especially to our Christian brothers and sisters.

Galatians 6:10 NLT

I tell you the truth, whatever you did for one of the least of these brothers of mine, you did for me.

Matthew 25:40 NIV

My Priorities for Life

I understand the need to give generously with my time.

I understand the importance of being a cheerful giver.

I understand the importance of being a faithful steward of my talents.

Check Your Priority		
High	Med.	Low
—	—	—
—	—	—
—	—	—

Mountain-moving Faith

Be on the alert, stand firm in the faith, act like men, be strong.

1 Corinthians 16:13 NASB

Because we live in a demanding world, all of us have mountains to climb and mountains to move. Moving those mountains requires faith.

Are you a mountain-moving guy or girl whose faith is evident for all to see? Or, are you a spiritual underachiever? As you think about the answer to that question, consider this: God needs more people who are willing to move mountains for His glory and for His kingdom.

Every life—including yours—is a series of wins and loses. Every step of the way, through every triumph and tragedy, God walks with you, ready and willing to strengthen you. So the next time you find your courage tested to the limit, remember to take your fears to God. If you call upon Him, you will be comforted. Whatever your challenge, whatever your trouble, God can handle it.

When you place your faith, your trust, indeed your life in the hands of your Heavenly Father, you'll be amazed at the marvelous things He can do with you and through you. So strengthen your faith through praise, through worship, through

Bible study, and through prayer. And trust God's plans. With Him, all things are possible, and He stands ready to open a world of possibilities to you . . . if you have faith.

And now, with no more delays, let the mountain moving begin.

I am truly grateful that faith enables me to move past the question of "Why?"

Zig Ziglar

PRIORITIES FOR MY LIFE

Faith should be practiced more than studied. Vance Havner said, "Nothing is more disastrous than to study faith, analyze faith, make noble resolves of faith, but never actually to make the leap of faith." How true!

TIMELESS WISDOM FOR GODLY LIVING

Where reason cannot wade, there faith must swim.

Thomas Watson

I want my life to be a faith-filled leap into his arms, knowing he will be there—not that everything will go as I want, but that he will be there and that this will be enough.

Sheila Walsh

Faith is trusting in advance what will only make sense in reverse.

Phillip Yancey

Faith is the quiet place within us where we don't get whiplash every time life tosses us a curve.

Patsy Clairmont

For whatever is born of God overcomes the world. And this is the victory that has overcome the world—our faith.
1 John 5:4 NKJV

Let me encourage you to continue to wait with faith. God may not perform a miracle, but He is trustworthy to touch you and make you whole where there used to be a hole.

Lisa Whelchel

MORE WORDS FROM GOD'S WORD

Fight the good fight of faith; take hold of the eternal life to which you were called . . . .

1 Timothy 6:12 NASB

Therefore, being always of good courage . . . we walk by faith, not by sight.

2 Corinthians 5:6-7 NASB

I have fought the good fight, I have finished the race, I have kept the faith.

2 Timothy 4:7 NIV

Anything is possible if you have faith.

Mark 9:23 TLB

My Priorities for Life

I trust that God can do big things . . . and I will expect that God will do big things.

I am determined to seek God's will and to follow God's Son.

I will praise God many times each day for His blessings.

I will build my faith each day through regular Bible study and prayer.

Check Your Priority		
High	Med.	Low
—	—	—
—	—	—
—	—	—
—	—	—

The Dating Game

Do not be unequally yoked together with unbelievers.
For what fellowship has righteousness with lawlessness?
And what communion has light with darkness?

2 Corinthians 6:14 NKJV

Is God a part of your dating life? Hopefully so. If you sincerely want to know God, then you should date people who feel the same way.

If you're still searching for Mr. or Mrs. Right (while trying to avoid falling in love with Mr. or Mrs. Wrong), be patient, be prudent, and be picky. Look for someone whose values you respect, whose behavior you approve of, and whose faith you admire. Remember that appearances can be deceiving and tempting, so watch your step. And when it comes to the important task of building a lifetime relationship with the guy or girl of your dreams, pray about it!

If you happen to be one of those very lucky ones who has already fallen madly in love with the same wonderful person who has (praise the Lord!) already fallen madly in love with you, say a great big thanks to the Matchmaker in heaven. But if you haven't yet found a soul-mate who honors both you and God, don't fret. Just keep trusting your Father in heaven, and keep yourself open to the direction in which He is leading you. And remember: When it comes to your dating life, God wants to give

His approval—or not—but He won't give it until He's asked. So ask, listen, and decide accordingly.

It is possible to be close to people physically and miles away from them spiritually.

Warren Wiersbe

We discover our role in life through our relationships with others.

Rick Warren

PRIORITIES FOR MY LIFE

Be choosy: Don't "settle" for second-class treatment—you deserve someone who values you as a person . . . and shows it.

TIMELESS WISDOM FOR GODLY LIVING

Living life with a consistent spiritual walk deeply influences those we love most.

Vonette Bright

I have decided not to let my time be used up by people to whom I make no difference while I neglect those for whom I am irreplaceable.

Tony Campolo

If God has you in the palm of his hand and your real life is secure in him, then you can venture forth—into the places and relationships, the challenges, the very heart of the storm—and you will be safe there.

Paula Rinehart

> *Love does no harm to its neighbor.*
> *Therefore love is the fulfillment of the law.*
> Romans 13:10 NIV

With resolve that you are going to make a relationship work, you can develop peace treaties of love and tolerance and harmony to transform a difficult situation into something beautiful.

Max Lucado

MORE WORDS FROM GOD'S WORD

Thine own friend, and thy father's friend, forsake not . . . .

Proverbs 27:10 KJV

Carry each other's burdens, and in this way you will fulfill the law of Christ.

Galatians 6:2 NIV

And be kind to one another, tenderhearted, forgiving one another, just as God in Christ forgave you.

Ephesians 4:32 NKJV

How wonderful, how beautiful, when brothers and sisters get along!

Psalm 133:1 MSG

My Priorities for Life

In my dating life, I go places where I am likely to bump into the kind of people I want to meet.

In my dating life, I desire to glorify God so I pray for His guidance, and follow it.

I don't feel compelled to date "just for the sake of dating." I believe that it's better to be dating nobody than to be dating the wrong person.

Check Your Priority		
High	Med.	Low
—	—	—
—	—	—
—	—	—

The Power of Patience

Knowing God leads to self-control. Self-control leads to patient endurance, and patient endurance leads to godliness.

2 Peter 1:6 NLT

Most of us are impatient for God to grant us the desires of our heart. Usually, we know what we want, and we know precisely when we want it: right now, if not sooner. But God may have other plans. And when God's plans differ from our own, we must trust in His infinite wisdom and in His infinite love.

As busy guys and girls living in a fast-paced world, many of us find that waiting quietly for God is difficult. Why? Because we are imperfect human beings seeking to live according to our own timetables, not God's. In our better moments, we realize that patience is not only a virtue, but it is also a commandment from the Creator.

God instructs us to be patient in all things. We must be patient with our families, with our friends, and with our acquaintances. We must also be patient with our Heavenly Father as He unfolds His plan for our lives. And that's as it should be. After all, think how patient God has been with us.

When I am dealing with an all-powerful, all-knowing God,
I, as a mere mortal, must offer my petitions not only
with persistence, but also with patience.
Someday I'll know why.

Ruth Bell Graham

Patience and encouragement come from God.
And I pray that God will help you all agree with each other
the way Christ Jesus wants.

Romans 15:5 NCV

PRIORITIES FOR MY LIFE

The best things in life seldom happen overnight . . . Henry
Blackaby writes, "The grass that is here today and gone tomorrow
does not require much time to mature. A big oak tree that lasts
for generations requires much more time to grow and mature.
God is concerned about your life through eternity. Allow Him to
take all the time He needs to shape you for His purposes. Larger
assignments will require longer periods of preparation." How
true!

TIMELESS WISDOM FOR GODLY LIVING

We must never think that patience is complacency. Patience is endurance in action.

Warren Wiersbe

God is never in a hurry.

Oswald Chambers

The next time you're disappointed, don't panic and don't give up. Just be patient and let God remind you he's still in control.

Max Lucado

When life is difficult, God wants us to have a faith that trusts and waits.

Kay Arthur

Now we exhort you, brethren, warn those who are unruly, comfort the fainthearted, uphold the weak, be patient with all.
1 Thessalonians 5:14 NKJV

Wisdom always waits for the right time to act, while emotion always pushes for action right now.

Joyce Meyer

MORE WORDS FROM GOD'S WORD

Patience of spirit is better than haughtiness of spirit.

Ecclesiastes 7:8 NASB

God has chosen you and made you his holy people. He loves you. So always do these things: Show mercy to others, be kind, humble, gentle, and patient.

Colossians 3:12 NCV

But if we look forward to something we don't have yet, we must wait patiently and confidently.

Romans 8:25 NLT

My Priorities for Life

Even when I don't understand the circumstances that confront me, I strive to wait patiently while serving the Lord.

I take seriously the Bible's instructions to be patient.

I believe that patience is not idle waiting but that it is an activity that means being watchful as I wait for God to lead me.

Check Your Priority		
High	Med.	Low
—	—	—
—	—	—
—	—	—

Valuing God's Word

Every word of God is pure: he is a shield unto them that put their trust in him.

Proverbs 30:5 KJV

Too many Christians treat the Bible like any other book. But get this loud and clear: THE BIBLE ISN'T LIKE ANY OTHER BOOK! Period! And if you're wise, you'll give your Bible the reverence and the attention that it deserves.

Is God's Word a bright spotlight that guides your path, or is it a tiny night light that occasionally flickers? Is God's Word your indispensable compass for everyday living, or is it relegated to Sunday morning services? Do you read the Bible faithfully or sporadically? The answer to these questions will determine the direction of your thoughts, the direction of your day, and the direction of your life.

George Mueller observed, "The vigor of our spiritual lives will be in exact proportion to the place held by the Bible in our lives and in our thoughts." Think of it like this: the more you use your Bible, the more God will use you.

God's Word can be a road map to a place of righteousness and abundance. Make it your road map. God's wisdom can be a light to guide your steps. Claim it as your light today, tomorrow, and every day of your life—and then walk confidently in the footsteps of God's only begotten Son.

Unless we form the habit of going to the Bible in bright moments as well as in trouble, we cannot fully respond to its consolations because we lack equilibrium between light and darkness.

Helen Keller

PRIORITIES FOR MY LIFE

Trust God's Word: Charles Swindoll writes, "There are four words I wish we would never forget, and they are, 'God keeps his word.'" And remember this: When it comes to studying God's Word, school is always in session.

TIMELESS WISDOM FOR GODLY LIVING

Don't worry about what you do not understand of the Bible.
Worry about what you do understand and do not live by.

Corrie ten Boom

The Bible is better documented than ancient history!

Charles Stanley

Nobody ever outgrows Scripture; the book widens and deepens
with our years.

C. H. Spurgeon

If a man's Bible is coming apart, it is an indication that he himself
is fairly well put together.

James Jennings

*Blessed are those who hunger and thirst for righteousness,
for they will be filled.*
Matthew 5:6 NIV

The Bible plainly teaches that if we will learn and act on the
Word, God will bless our lives.

Joyce Meyer

MORE WORDS FROM GOD'S WORD

For the word of God is quick, and powerful, and sharper than any two-edged sword, piercing even to the dividing asunder of soul and spirit, and of the joints and marrow, and is a discerner of the thoughts and intents of the heart.

Hebrews 4:12 KJV

Man shall not live by bread alone, but by every word that proceeds from the mouth of God.

Matthew 4:4 NKJV

For I am not ashamed of the gospel, because it is God's power for salvation to everyone who believes.

Romans 1:16 Holman CSB

My Priorities for Life

	Check Your Priority		
	High	Med.	Low
I have a regular time when I study the Bible and meditate upon its meaning for my life.	—	—	—
When my behavior is inconsistent with God's Word, I understand the need to change my behavior.	—	—	—
I value the Bible as God's Word, and I believe that the Bible is true.	—	—	—

Why Worship?

A time is coming and has now come when the true worshipers
will worship the Father in spirit and truth, for they are the kind of
worshipers the Father seeks. God is spirit, and his worshipers
must worship in spirit and in truth.

John 4:23-24 NIV

Here's a simple question: Why do you attend church? Is it because of your sincere desire to worship and to praise God? Hopefully you can honestly answer yes. Yet, far too many Christians attend worship services because they believe they are "supposed to go to church" or because they feel "pressured" to attend. Still others go to church for "social" reasons. But make no mistake: the best reason to attend church is out of a sincere desire to please God, to praise God, to experience God, and to discern God's will for your life.

Some people may tell you that they don't engage in worship. Don't believe them. All of mankind is engaged in worship. The question is not whether we worship, but what we worship. Wise girls and guys choose to worship God. When they do, they are blessed with a plentiful harvest of joy, peace, and abundance. Other people choose to distance themselves from God by foolishly worshiping things that are intended to bring personal gratification but not spiritual gratification. Such choices often have tragic consequences.

How can we ensure that we cast our lot with God? We do so, in part, by the practice of regular, purposeful worship in the company of fellow believers. When we worship God faithfully and fervently, we are blessed. When we fail to worship God, for whatever reason, we forfeit the spiritual gifts that might otherwise be ours.

We must worship our heavenly Father, not just with our words, but also with our deeds. We must honor Him, praise Him, and obey Him. As we seek to find purpose and meaning for our lives, we must first seek His purpose and His will. For believers, God comes first. Always first.

The most common mistake Christians make in worship today is seeking an experience rather than seeking God.

Rick Warren

PRIORITIES FOR MY LIFE

The best way to worship God . . . is to worship Him sincerely and often.

TIMELESS WISDOM FOR GODLY LIVING

It's our privilege to not only raise our hands in worship but also to combine the visible with the invisible in a rising stream of praise and adoration sent directly to our Father.

Shirley Dobson

Worship is our response to the overtures of love from the heart of the Father.

Richard Foster

Worship is about rekindling an ashen heart into a blazing fire.

Liz Curtis Higgs

If any man thirst, let him come unto me, and drink.
John 7:37 KJV

In the sanctuary, we discover beauty: the beauty of His presence.

Kay Arthur

The fact that we were created to enjoy God and to worship him forever is etched upon our souls.

Jim Cymbala

MORE WORDS FROM GOD'S WORD

For it is written, "You shall worship the Lord your God, and Him only you shall serve."

Matthew 4:10 NKJV

But seek first his kingdom and his righteousness, and all these things will be given to you as well.

Matthew 6:33 NIV

God lifted him high and honored him far beyond anyone or anything, ever, so that all created beings in heaven and earth, even those long ago dead and buried, will bow in worship before this Jesus Christ, and call out in praise that he is the Master of all, to the glorious honor of God the Father.

Philippians 2:9-11 MSG

My Priorities for Life

	Check Your Priority		
	High	Med.	Low
I consider praise and worship to be a regular part of my day.	—	—	—
I sincerely want to worship God in spirit and truth.	—	—	—
I understand the importance of being actively involved in my church.	—	—	—
I consider each day an opportunity to praise God and to worship Him.	—	—	—

Walking in Truth

Therefore laying aside falsehood, speak truth, each one of you,
with his neighbor, for we are members of one another.

Ephesians 4:25 NASB

Hey, would you like a time-tested, ironclad formula for success? Here it is: guard your integrity like you guard your wallet.

It has been said on many occasions and in many ways that honesty is the best policy. For Christians, it is far more important to note that honesty is God's policy. And if we are to be servants worthy of our Savior, Jesus Christ, we must be honest, forthright, and trustworthy.

Telling the truth means telling the whole truth. And that means summoning the courage to deliver bad news when necessary. And for some of us, especially those of us who are card-carrying people pleasers, telling the whole truth can be difficult indeed (especially if we're pretty sure that the truth will make somebody mad). Still, if we wish to fashion successful lives, we've got to learn to be totally truthful—part-time truth-telling doesn't cut the mustard.

Sometimes, honesty is difficult; sometimes, honesty is painful; sometimes, honesty is inconvenient; but honesty is always God's way. In the Book of Proverbs, we read, "The Lord detests lying lips, but he delights in men who are truthful" (12:22 NIV). Clearly, truth is God's way, and it must be our way, too, even when telling the truth is difficult.

Only Jesus Christ is the truth for everyone who has ever been born into the human race, regardless of culture, age, nationality, generation, heritage, gender, color, or language.

Anne Graham Lotz

PRIORITIES FOR MY LIFE

Know the truth . . . and live it: Warren Wiersbe writes, "Learning God's truth and getting it into our heads is one thing, but living God's truth and getting it into our characters is quite something else." So don't be satisfied to sit on the sidelines and observe the truth at a distance—live it.

TIMELESS WISDOM FOR GODLY LIVING

Those who walk in truth walk in liberty.

Beth Moore

We have in Jesus Christ a perfect example of how to put God's truth into practice.

Bill Bright

Having a doctrine pass before the mind is not what the Bible means by knowing the truth. It's only when it reaches down deep into the heart that the truth begins to set us free, just as a key must penetrate a lock to turn it, or as rainfall must saturate the earth down to the roots in order for your garden to grow.

John Eldredge

Jesus answered, "I am the way and the truth and the life. No one comes to the Father except through me."
John 14:6 NIV

There is a balance to be maintained in situations. That balance is the Holy Spirit within us to guide us into the truth of each situation and circumstance in which we find ourselves. He will provide us the wisdom to know when we are to be adaptable and adjustable and when we are to take a firm stand and be immovable.

Joyce Meyer

MORE WORDS FROM GOD'S WORD

A person who does not have the Spirit does not accept the truths that come from the Spirit of God. That person thinks they are foolish and cannot understand them, because they can only be judged to be true by the Spirit. The spiritual person is able to judge all things, but no one can judge him.

1 Corinthians 2:14–15 NCV

This and this only has been my appointed work: getting this news to those who have never heard of God, and explaining how it works by simple faith and plain truth.

1 Timothy 2:7 MSG

For God's wrath is revealed from heaven against all godlessness and unrighteousness of people who by their unrighteousness suppress the truth.

Romans 1:18 Holman CSB

My Priorities for Life

I believe unless I build my relationships on honesty, I'm building on a slippery, sandy slope.

I believe even when telling the truth is hard, it's always the right thing to do.

I believe that little white lies become king-sized ones.

	Check Your Priority	
High	Med.	Low
—	—	—
—	—	—
—	—	—

Materialism 101: The Value of Stuff

Do not love the world or the things in the world.
If anyone loves the world, the love of the Father is not in him.

1 John 2:15 NKJV

Is "shop till you drop" your motto? Hopefully not. On the grand stage of a well-lived life, material possessions should play a rather small role. Of course, we all need the basic necessities of life, but once we meet those needs, the piling up of stuff creates more problems than it solves.

Our society is in love with money and the things that money can buy. God is not. God cares about people, not possessions, and so must we. We must, to the best of our abilities, love our neighbors as ourselves, and we must, to the best of our abilities, resist the mighty temptation to place possessions ahead of people.

How much stuff is too much stuff? Well, if your desire for stuff is getting in the way of your desire to know God, then you've got too much stuff—it's as simple as that.

If you find yourself wrapped up in the concerns of the material world, it's time to reorder your priorities by turning your thoughts to more important matters. And, it's time to begin storing up riches that will endure throughout eternity: the spiritual kind. Money, in and of itself, is not evil; worshipping money is. So today, as you prioritize matters of importance in your life, remember that God is almighty, but the dollar is not.

The more we stuff ourselves
with material pleasures,
the less we seem to appreciate life.

Barbara Johnson

PRIORITIES FOR MY LIFE

Materialism Made Simple: The world wants you to believe that "money and stuff" can buy happiness. Don't believe it! Genuine happiness comes not from money, but from the things that money can't buy—starting, of course, with your relationship to God and His only begotten Son.

TIMELESS WISDOM FOR GODLY LIVING

We are made spiritually lethargic by a steady diet of materialism.

Mary Morrison Suggs

The socially prescribed affluent, middle-class lifestyle has become so normative in our churches that we discern little conflict between it and the Christian lifestyle prescribed in the New Testament.

Tony Campolo

There is absolutely no evidence that complexity and materialism lead to happiness. On the contrary, there is plenty of evidence that simplicity and spirituality lead to joy, a blessedness that is better than happiness.

Dennis Swanberg

He who trusts in his riches will fall,
but the righteous will flourish . . . .
Proverbs 11:28 NKJV

The Scriptures also reveal a warning that if we are consumed with greed, not only do we disobey God, but we will miss the opportunity to allow Him to use us as instruments for others.

Charles Stanley

MORE WORDS FROM GOD'S WORD

For what will it profit a man if he gains the whole world, and loses his own soul? Or what will a man give in exchange for his soul?

Mark 8:36-37 NKJV

For where your treasure is, there your heart will be also.

Luke 12:34 NKJV

Since we entered the world penniless and will leave it penniless, if we have bread on the table and shoes on our feet, that's enough.

1 Timothy 6:7-8 MSG

For the mind-set of the flesh is death, but the mind-set of the Spirit is life and peace.

Romans 8:6 Holman CSB

My Priorities for Life

My spending habits reflect the values that I hold most dear, so I try my best to be a faithful steward of my resources.

I believe that my possessions are actually God's possessions, so I try to use them for His purposes.

I don't expect material possessions to bring me lasting happiness.

Check Your Priority		
High	Med.	Low
—	—	—
—	—	—
—	—	—

Speaking With a Voice of Triumph

For You have made him a little lower than the angels,
And You have crowned him with glory and honor.

Psalm 8:5 NKJV

Are you your own worst critic? If so, it's time to become a little more understanding of the person you see whenever you look into the mirror.

Millions of words have been written about various ways to improve self-image and increase self-esteem. Yet, maintaining a healthy self-image is, to a surprising extent, a matter of doing three things: 1. Obeying God 2. Thinking healthy thoughts 3. Finding a purpose for your life that pleases your Creator and yourself.

The following common-sense, Biblically-based tips can help you build the kind of self-image—and the kind of life—that both you and God can be proud of:

Do the right thing: If you're misbehaving, how can you possibly hope to feel good about yourself? (See Romans 14:12)

Watch what you think: If your inner voice is, in reality, your inner critic, you need to tone down the criticism now. And while you're at it, train yourself to begin thinking thoughts that are more rational, more accepting, and less judgmental. (Philippians 4:8)

Spend time with boosters, not critics: Are your friends putting you down? If so, find new friends. (Hebrews 3:13)

Find something that you're passionate about: Become so busy following your passion that you forget to worry about your self-esteem. (Colossians 3:23)

Don't worry too much about self-esteem. Instead, worry more about living a life that is pleasing to God. Learn to think optimistically. Find a worthy purpose. Find people to love and people to serve. When you do, your self-esteem will, on most days, take care of itself.

Being loved by Him whose opinion matters most gives us the security to risk loving, too—even loving ourselves.

Gloria Gaither

PRIORITIES FOR MY LIFE

You are incredibly special to God . . . Are you incredibly special to yourself?

TIMELESS WISDOM FOR GODLY LIVING

Believe in yourself. Have faith in your abilities. Without a humble but reasonable confidence in your own powers, you can't be successful or happy.

Norman Vincent Peale

As I have grown in faith and confidence, I have known more and more that my worth is based on the love of God.

Leslie Williams

You are valuable just because you exist. Not because of what you do or what you have done, but simply because you are.

Max Lucado

You are valuable because God values you.

Stanley Grenz

How happy are those whose way is blameless, who live according to the law of the Lord! Happy are those who keep His decrees and seek Him with all their heart.
Psalm 119:1-2 Holman CSB

A healthy self-identity is seeing yourself as God sees you—no more and no less.

Josh McDowell

MORE WORDS FROM GOD'S WORD

Happy is the one whose help is the God of Jacob, whose hope is in the Lord his God.

Psalm 146:5 Holman CSB

If God is for us, who is against us?

Romans 8:31 Holman CSB

Finally, brethren, whatever things are true, whatever things are noble, whatever things are just, whatever things are pure, whatever things are lovely, whatever things are of good report, if there is any virtue and if there is anything praiseworthy—meditate on these things.

Philippians 4:8 NKJV

My Priorities for Life

I trust that God is working in me and through me to help me become the person He intends for me to be.

I believe that one reason to study God's Word is this: It tells me what God thinks of my life.

Because I know that God loves me, I believe that I should love myself.

Check Your Priority		
High	Med.	Low
—	—	—
—	—	—
—	—	—

Putting Off Till Tomorrow

If you do nothing in a difficult time, your strength is limited.

Proverbs 24:10 Holman CSB

When something important needs to be done, the best time to do it is sooner rather than later. But sometimes, instead of doing the smart thing (which, by the way, is choosing "sooner"), we may choose "later." When we do, we may pay a heavy price for our shortsightedness.

The habit of procrastination takes a two-fold toll on its victims. First, important work goes unfinished; second (and more importantly), valuable energy is wasted in the process of putting off the things that remain undone. Procrastination results from an individual's short-sighted attempt to postpone temporary discomfort. What results is a senseless cycle of 1. Delay, followed by 2. Worry, followed by 3. A panicky and futile attempt to "catch up." Procrastination is, at its core, a struggle against oneself; the only antidote is action.

Once you acquire the habit of doing what needs to be done when it needs to be done, you will avoid untold trouble, worry, and stress. So learn to defeat procrastination by paying less attention to your fears and more attention to your responsibilities.

Are you one of those people who puts things off till the last minute? If so, it's time to change your ways. Whatever "it" is, do it now. When you do, you won't have to worry about "it" later.

Not now becomes never.

Martin Luther

PRIORITIES FOR MY LIFE

It's easy to put off unpleasant tasks until "later." A far better strategy is this: Do the unpleasant work first so you can enjoy the rest of the day.

TIMELESS WISDOM FOR GODLY LIVING

Character is formed by doing the thing we are supposed to do, when it should be done, whether we feel like doing it or not.

Father Flanagan

Do noble things, do not dream them all day long.

Charles Kingsley

Do the unpleasant work first and enjoy the rest of the day.

Marie T. Freeman

I've found that the worst thing I can do when it comes to any kind of potential pressure situation is to put off dealing with it.

John Maxwell

If you are too lazy to plow in the right season, you will have no food at the harvest.
Proverbs 20:4 NLT

I cannot fix what I will not face.

Jim Gallery

MORE WORDS FROM GOD'S WORD

When you make a vow to God, do not delay in fulfilling it. He has no pleasure in fools; fulfill your vow.

Ecclesiastes 5:4 NIV

We can't afford to waste a minute, must not squander these precious daylight hours in frivolity and indulgence, in sleeping around and dissipation, in bickering and grabbing everything in sight. Get out of bed and get dressed! Don't loiter and linger, waiting until the very last minute. Dress yourselves in Christ, and be up and about!

Romans 13:13-14 MSG

Now, Lord, what do I wait for? My hope is in You.

Psalm 39:7 Holman CSB

My Priorities for Life

Since I believe that procrastination only delays the inevitable, I try to do things sooner rather than later.

I understand the importance of doing first things first, even if I'd rather be doing something else.

I try to avoid the trap of procrastination because I know that procrastination is counterproductive to my own best interests.

Check Your Priority		
High	Med.	Low
—	—	—
—	—	—
—	—	—

The Company You Keep

He who walks with wise men will be wise,
but the companion of fools will be destroyed.

Proverbs 13:20 NKJV

Are you a people-pleaser or a God-pleaser? Hopefully, you're far more concerned with pleasing God than you are with pleasing your friends. But even if you're a devoted Christian, you may, from time to time, feel the urge to impress your friends and acquaintances—and sometimes that urge will be strong.

Peer pressure can be good or bad, depending upon who your peers are and how they behave. If your friends encourage you to follow God's will and to obey His commandments, then you'll experience positive peer pressure, and that's a good thing. But, if your friends encourage you to do foolish things, then you're facing a different kind of peer pressure . . . and you'd better beware. When you feel pressured to do things—or to say things—that lead you away from God, you're heading straight for trouble. So don't do the "easy" thing or the "popular" thing. Do the right thing, and don't worry about winning any popularity contests.

Are you satisfied to follow the crowd? If so, you will probably pay a heavy price for your shortsightedness. But if you're determined to follow the One from Galilee, He will guide your steps and bless your undertakings. To sum it up, here's your choice: you can choose to please God first, or you can fall prey to peer pressure. The choice is yours—and so are the consequences.

You will get untold flak for prioritizing God's revealed and present will for your life over man's . . . but, boy, is it worth it.

Beth Moore

Do not be misled: "Bad company corrupts good character."

1 Corinthians 15:33 NIV

PRIORITIES FOR MY LIFE

Put peer pressure to work for you. How? By associating with people who, by their actions and their words, will encourage you to become a better person.

TIMELESS WISDOM FOR GODLY LIVING

Do you want to be wise? Choose wise friends.

Charles Swindoll

There is nothing that makes more cowards and feeble men than public opinion.

Henry Ward Beecher

Comparison is the root of all feelings of inferiority.

James Dobson

I have found that the closer I am to the godly people around me, the easier it is for me to live a righteous life because they hold me accountable.

John MacArthur

For am I now trying to win the favor of people, or God? Or am I striving to please people? If I were still trying to please people, I would not be a slave of Christ.
Galatians 1:10 Holman CSB

True friends will always lift you higher and challenge you to walk in a manner pleasing to our Lord.

Lisa Bevere

MORE WORDS FROM GOD'S WORD

Stay away from a foolish man; you will gain no knowledge from his speech.

Proverbs 14:7 Holman CSB

My son, if sinners entice you, don't be persuaded.

Proverbs 1:10 Holman CSB

Blessed is the man who walks not in the counsel of the ungodly, nor stands in the path of sinners, nor sits in the seat of the scornful; but his delight is in the law of the Lord, and in His law he meditates day and night.

Psalm 1:1-2 NKJV

Don't become partners with those who reject God. How can you make a partnership out of right and wrong? That's not partnership; that's war. Is light best friends with dark?

2 Corinthians 6:14 MSG

My Priorities for Life

| | Check Your Priority | |
High	Med.	Low

I actively seek out wise friends who help me make right choices.

— — —

I understand that being obedient to God means that I cannot always please other people.

— — —

I understand the importance of pleasing God first.

— — —

Obedience to the Ultimate Authority

It is the LORD your God you must follow, and him you must revere.
Keep his commands and obey him;
serve him and hold fast to him.

Deuteronomy 13:4 NIV

Obedience to God is determined, not by words, but by deeds. Talking about righteousness is easy; living righteously is far more difficult, especially in today's temptation-filled world.

Since God created Adam and Eve, we human beings have been rebelling against our Creator. Why? Because we are unwilling to trust God's Word, and we are unwilling to follow His commandments. God has given us a guidebook for righteous living called the Holy Bible. It contains thorough instructions which, if followed, lead to fulfillment, abundance, and salvation. But, if we choose to ignore God's commandments, the results are as predictable as they are tragic.

In Ephesians 2:10 we read, "For we are His workmanship, created in Christ Jesus for good works" (NKJV). These words are instructive: We are not saved by good works, but for good works. Good works are not the root but, rather, the fruit of our salvation.

When we seek righteousness in our own lives—and when we seek the companionship of those who do likewise—we reap the spiritual rewards that God intends for our lives. When we behave ourselves as godly men and women, we honor God. When we live righteously and according to God's commandments, He blesses us in ways that we cannot fully understand.

Do you seek God's peace and His blessings? Then obey Him. When you're faced with a difficult choice or a powerful temptation, seek God's counsel and trust the counsel He gives. Invite God into your heart and live according to His commandments. When you do, you will be blessed today and tomorrow and forever.

God is God. Because He is God, He is worthy of my trust and obedience. I will find rest nowhere but in His holy will, a will that is unspeakably beyond my largest notions of what He is up to.

Elisabeth Elliot

PRIORITIES FOR MY LIFE

Obedience leads to spiritual growth: Anne Graham Lotz correctly observed, "If you want to discover your spiritual gifts, start obeying God. As you serve Him, you will find that He has given you the gifts that are necessary to follow through in obedience."

TIMELESS WISDOM FOR GODLY LIVING

Obedience that is not motivated by love cannot produce the spiritual fruit that God wants from His children.

Warren Wiersbe

We offend God if we feel that he is cheating us out of life, as if obeying him were a fast rather than a feast. Obedience is a privilege not granted to everyone. After all, God "comes to the help" of obedient people.

Raymond Ortlund

When we choose deliberately to obey Him, then He will tax the remotest star and the last grain of sand to assist us with all His almighty power.

Oswald Chambers

The world and its desires pass away, but the man who does the will of God lives forever.
1 John 2:17 NIV

Compared to God's part, our part is minuscule but necessary. We don't have to do much, but we have to do something.

Max Lucado

MORE WORDS FROM GOD'S WORD

Does the LORD delight in burnt offerings and sacrifices as much as in obeying the voice of the LORD? To obey is better than sacrifice . . . .

1 Samuel 15:22 NIV

Peter and the other apostles replied: "We must obey God rather than men!"

Acts 5:29 NIV

If they obey and serve him, they will spend the rest of their days in prosperity and their years in contentment.

Job 36:11 NIV

For it is not those who hear the law who are righteous in God's sight, but it is those who obey the law who will be declared righteous.

Romans 2:13 NIV

My Priorities for Life

When I obey God, I feel better about myself.

I understand that my obedience to God is a demonstration of the gratitude that I feel in my heart for the blessings I have been given.

Obedience to God may not always be easy or pleasant, but it is always satisfying.

Check Your Priority		
High	Med.	Low
—	—	—
—	—	—
—	—	—

Valuing God's Guidance

The Lord says, "I will make you wise and show you where to go.
I will guide you and watch over you."

Psalm 32:8 NCV

When we genuinely seek to know God's will—when we prayerfully seek His wisdom and His guidance—our Heavenly Father carefully leads us over the peaks and valleys of life. And as Christians, we can be comforted: Whether we find ourselves at the pinnacle of the mountain or the darkest depths of the valley, God is always there with us.

C. S. Lewis observed, "I don't doubt that the Holy Spirit guides your decisions from within when you make them with the intention of pleasing God. The error would be to think that He speaks only within, whereas in reality He speaks also through Scripture, the Church, Christian friends, and books." These words remind us that God has many ways to make Himself known. Our challenge is to make ourselves open to His instruction.

Do you place a high value on God's guidance, and do you talk to Him regularly about matters great and small? Or do you talk with God on a haphazard basis? If you're wise, you'll form the habit of speaking to God early and often. But you won't stop there—you'll also study God's Word, you'll obey God's commandments, and you'll associate with people who do likewise.

So, if you're unsure of your next step, lean upon God's promises and lift your prayers to Him. Remember that God is always near—always trying to get His message through. Open yourself to Him every day, and trust Him to guide your path. When you do, you'll be protected today, tomorrow, and forever.

Are you serious about wanting God's guidance
to become a personal reality in your life?
The first step is to tell God that you know
you can't manage your own life;
that you need His help.

Catherine Marshall

PRIORITIES FOR MY LIFE

Need guidance? Pray for it. When you seek it, He will give it.

TIMELESS WISDOM FOR GODLY LIVING

God's guidance is even more important than common sense. I can declare that the deepest darkness is outshone by the light of Jesus.

Corrie ten Boom

Experience has taught me that the Shepherd is far more willing to show His sheep the path than the sheep are to follow. He is endlessly merciful, patient, tender, and loving. If we, His stupid and wayward sheep, really want to be led, we will without fail be led. Of that I am sure.

Elisabeth Elliot

A spiritual discipline is necessary in order to move slowly from an absurd to an obedient life, from a life filled with noisy worries to a life in which there is some free inner space where we can listen to our God and follow his guidance.

Henri Nouwen

> *The true children of God are those*
> *who let God's Spirit lead them.*
> *Romans 8:14 NCV*

God will prove to you how good and acceptable and perfect His will is when He's got His hands on the steering wheel of your life.

Stuart & Jill Briscoe

MORE WORDS FROM GOD'S WORD

Lord, You light my lamp; my God illuminates my darkness.

Psalm 18:28 Holman CSB

In all your ways acknowledge Him, and He shall direct your paths.

Proverbs 3:6 NKJV

Every morning he wakes me. He teaches me to listen like a student. The Lord God helps me learn . . .

Isaiah 50:4-5 NCV

I know the Lord is always with me. I will not be shaken, for he is right beside me.

Psalm 16:8 NLT

My Priorities for Life

I understand the importance of seeking God's wisdom and His guidance.

I understand that whenever I genuinely trust God to guide my path, I will be comforted.

I allow God to guide me by His Word and by His Spirit.

Check Your Priority		
High	Med.	Low
—	—	—
—	—	—
—	—	—

The Temple of God That Belongs to You

Therefore, brothers, by the mercies of God,
I urge you to present your bodies as a living sacrifice,
holy and pleasing to God; this is your spiritual worship.

Romans 12:1 Holman CSB

How do you treat your body? Do you treat it with the reverence and respect it deserves, or do you take it more or less for granted? Well, the Bible has clear instructions about the way you should take care of the miraculous body that God has given you.

God's Word teaches us that our bodies are "temples" which belong to God (1 Corinthians 6:19-20). We are commanded (not encouraged, not advised—we are commanded!) to treat our bodies with respect and honor. We do so by making wise choices and by making those choices consistently over an extended period of time.

Do you sincerely seek to improve the overall quality of your life and your health? Then promise yourself—and God—that you will begin making the kind of wise choices that will lead to a longer, healthier, happier life. The responsibility for those choices is yours. And so are the rewards.

God wants you to give Him your body.
Some people do foolish things with their bodies.
God wants your body as a holy sacrifice.

Warren Wiersbe

Do you not know that your body is a sanctuary of the Holy Spirit who is in you, whom you have from God? You are not your own, for you were bought at a price; therefore glorify God in your body.

1 Corinthians 6:19-20 Holman CSB

PRIORITIES FOR MY LIFE

Fitness tips in the Bible: God's Word is full of advice about health, moderation, and sensible living. When you come across these passages, take them to heart and put them to use.

TIMELESS WISDOM FOR GODLY LIVING

Birds which are too heavy cannot fly very high. The same is true of those who mistreat their bodies.

St. John Climacus

The only way to keep your health is to eat what you don't want, drink what you don't like, and do what you'd rather not.

Mark Twain

If you desire to improve your physical well-being and your emotional outlook, increasing your faith can help you.

John Maxwell

Our primary motivation should not be for more energy or to avoid a heart attack but to please God with our bodies.

Carole Lewis

A cheerful disposition is good for your health; gloom and doom leave you bone-tired.
Proverbs 17:22 MSG

Our body is like armor, our soul like the warrior. Take care of both, and you will be ready for what comes.

Amma St. Syncletice

MORE WORDS FROM GOD'S WORD

They brought unto him all sick people that were taken with diverse diseases and torments . . . and he healed them.

Matthew 4:24 KJV

Is any among you afflicted? Let him pray.

James 5:13 KJV

Beloved, I pray that in all respects you may prosper and be in good health, just as your soul prospers.

3 John 1:2 NASB

For You formed my inward parts; You covered me in my mother's womb. I will praise You, for I am fearfully and wonderfully made; Marvelous are Your works.

Psalm 139:13-14 NKJV

My Priorities for Life

I believe God will help me become a more physically fit person if I will ask for His help.

I believe that God wants me to treat my body with care.

I understand the importance of staying physically fit.

Check Your Priority		
High	Med.	Low
—	—	—
—	—	—
—	—	—

A Willingness to Serve

So prepare your minds for service and have self-control.
All your hope should be for the gift of grace that will be yours
when Jesus Christ is shown to you.

1 Peter 1:13 NCV

The words of Jesus are clear: the most esteemed men and women in this world are not the big-shots who jump up on stage and hog the spotlight; the greatest among us are those who are willing to become humble servants.

Are you willing to become a servant for Christ? Are you willing to pitch in and make the world a better place, or are you determined to keep all your blessings to yourself? Hopefully, you are determined to follow Christ's example by making yourself an unselfish servant to those who need your help.

Today, you may be tempted to take more than you give. But if you feel the urge to be selfish, resist that urge with all your might. Don't be stingy, selfish, or self-absorbed. Instead, serve your friends quietly and without fanfare. Find a need and fill it . . . humbly. Lend a helping hand . . . anonymously. Share a word of kindness . . . with quiet sincerity. As you go about your daily activities, remember that the Savior of all humanity made Himself a servant, and we, as His followers, must do no less.

Service is the pathway to real significance.

Rick Warren

Whoever serves me must follow me.
Then my servant will be with me everywhere
I am. My Father will honor anyone
who serves me.

John 12:26 NCV

PRIORITIES FOR MY LIFE

Whatever your age, whatever your circumstances, you can serve: Each stage of life's journey is a glorious opportunity to place yourself in the service of the One who is the Giver of all blessings. As long as you live, you should honor God with your service to others.

TIMELESS WISDOM FOR GODLY LIVING

We can love Jesus in the hungry, the naked, and the destitute who are dying . . . If you love, you will be willing to serve. And you will find Jesus in the distressing disguise of the poor.

Mother Teresa

Christianity, in its purest form, is nothing more than seeing Jesus. Christian service, in its purest form, is nothing more than imitating him who we see. To see his Majesty and to imitate him: that is the sum of Christianity.

Max Lucado

God has lots of folks who intend to go to work for Him "some day." What He needs is more people who are willing to work for Him today.

Marie T. Freeman

There are different kinds of gifts, but they are all from the same Spirit. There are different ways to serve but the same Lord to serve.

1 Corinthians 12:4–5 NCV

God does not do anything with us, only through us.

Oswald Chambers

MORE WORDS FROM GOD'S WORD

Therefore, since we receive a kingdom which cannot be shaken, let us show gratitude, by which we may offer to God an acceptable service with reverence and awe . . . .

Hebrews 12:28 NASB

If they serve Him obediently, they will end their days in prosperity and their years in happiness.

Job 36:11 Holman CSB

We must do the works of Him who sent Me while it is day. Night is coming when no one can work.

John 9:4 Holman CSB

Serve the Lord with gladness.

Psalm 100:2 Holman CSB

My Priorities for Life

Greatness in God's kingdom relates to service, not status.

I am proactive in my search to find ways to help others.

Christ was a humble servant, and I value the importance of following His example.

Check Your Priority		
High	Med.	Low
—	—	—
—	—	—
—	—	—

Forgiving and Forgetting

Be even-tempered, content with second place, quick to forgive an offense.
Forgive as quickly and completely as the Master forgave you.
And regardless of what else you put on, wear love.
It's your basic, all-purpose garment. Never be without it.

Colossians 3:13-14 MSG

Are you the kind of person who has a tough time forgiving and forgetting? If so, welcome to the club. Most of us find it difficult to forgive the people who have hurt us. And that's too bad because life would be much simpler if we could forgive people "once and for all" and be done with it. Yet forgiveness is seldom that easy. Usually, the decision to forgive is straightforward, but the process of forgiving is more difficult. Forgiveness is a journey that requires effort, time, perseverance, and prayer.

If there exists even one person whom you have not forgiven (and that includes yourself), obey God's commandment: forgive that person today. And remember that bitterness, anger, and regret are not part of God's plan for your life. Forgiveness is.

If you sincerely wish to forgive someone, pray for that person. And then pray for yourself by asking God to heal your heart. Don't expect forgiveness to be easy or quick, but rest assured: with God as your partner, you can forgive . . . and you will.

If Jesus forgave those who nailed Him to the Cross,
and if God forgives you and me, how can you withhold
your forgiveness from someone else?

Anne Graham Lotz

Our Father is kind; you be kind. "Don't pick on people,
jump on their failures, criticize their faults—unless, of course,
you want the same treatment. Don't condemn those who are down;
that hardness can boomerang. Be easy on people;
you'll find life a lot easier."

Luke 6:36-37 MSG

PRIORITIES FOR MY LIFE

Holding a grudge? Drop it. Never expect other people to be more forgiving than you are. And remember: the best time to forgive is now.

TIMELESS WISDOM FOR GODLY LIVING

Only the truly forgiven are truly forgiving.

C. S. Lewis

We cannot out-sin God's ability to forgive us.

Beth Moore

It is said that forgiveness is the fragrance the violet sheds on the heel that has crushed it. If so, could there be a fragrance as sweet in all the Bible as that of Jesus washing the feet of the very one whose heel was raised against Him?

Charles Swindoll

Forgiveness is not an emotion. Forgiveness is an act of the will, and the will can function regardless of the temperature of the heart.

Corrie ten Boom

> *Be kind to one another, tender-hearted, forgiving each other, just as God in Christ also has forgiven you.*
> Ephesians 4:32 NASB

Give me such love for God and men as will blot out all hatred and bitterness.

Dietrich Bonhoeffer

MORE WORDS FROM GOD'S WORD

And forgive us our sins, for we ourselves also forgive everyone in debt to us. And do not bring us into temptation.

Luke 11:4 NKJV

Whenever you stand praying, forgive, if you have anything against anyone, so that your Father in heaven will also forgive you your transgressions.

Mark 11:25 NASB

Have mercy on me, O God, according to your unfailing love; according to your great compassion blot out my transgressions. Wash away all my iniquity and cleanse me from my sin.

Psalm 51:1-2 NIV

If you forgive those who sin against you, your heavenly Father will forgive you. But if you refuse to forgive others, your Father will not forgive your sins.

Matthew 6:14-15 NLT

My Priorities for Life

	Check Your Priority	
High	Med.	Low

Because God has forgiven me, I can forgive others.

—	—	—

Because God has forgiven me, I can forgive myself.

—	—	—

I understand that when I ask God for forgiveness, He grants it.

—	—	—

Possibilities According to God

*For His divine power has given us everything required for life
and godliness, through the knowledge of Him who called us
by His own glory and goodness.*

2 Peter 1:3 Holman CSB

We live in a world of infinite possibilities. But sometimes, because of limited faith and limited understanding, we wrongly assume that God cannot or will not intervene in the affairs of mankind. Such assumptions are simply wrong.

Are you afraid to ask God to do big things in your life? Is your faith threadbare and worn? If so, it's time to abandon your doubts and reclaim your faith—faith in yourself, faith in your abilities, faith in your future, and faith in your Heavenly Father.

Catherine Marshall notes that, "God specializes in things thought impossible." And make no mistake: God can help you do things you never dreamed possible . . . your job is to let Him.

Sometimes, when we read of God's miraculous works in Biblical times, we tell ourselves, "That was then, but this is now." When we do so, we are mistaken. God is with His children "now" just as He was "then." He is right here, right now, performing miracles. And, He will continue to work miracles in our lives to the extent that we are willing to trust in Him and to the extent that those miracles fit into the fabric of His divine plan.

Miracles—both great and small—happen around us all day every day, but usually, we're too busy to notice. Some miracles, like the twinkling of a star or the glory of a sunset, we take for granted. Other miracles, like the healing of a terminally sick patient, we chalk up to fate or to luck. We assume, quite incorrectly, that God is "out there" and we are "right here." Nothing could be farther from the truth.

Do you lack the faith that God can work miracles in your own life? If so, it's time to reconsider. Instead of doubting God, trust His power, and expect His miracles. Then, wait patiently . . . because something miraculous is about to happen.

The God who spoke still speaks.
He comes into our world.
He comes into your world.
He comes to do what you can't.

Max Lucado

PRIORITIES FOR MY LIFE

If you're looking for miracles . . . you'll find them. If you're not, you won't.

TIMELESS WISDOM FOR GODLY LIVING

The power of God through His Spirit will work within us to the degree that we permit it.

Mrs. Charles E. Cowman

As we join together in prayer, we draw on God's enabling might in a way that multiplies our own efforts many times over.

Shirley Dobson

He upholds the whole creation, founded the earth, and still sustains it by the word of his power. What cannot he do in the affairs of families and kingdoms, far beyond our conception and expectation, who hangs the earth upon nothing?

Matthew Henry

If we take God's program, we can have God's power—not otherwise.

E. Stanley Jones

For the LORD your God is God of gods and Lord of lords, the great God, mighty and awesome.
Deuteronomy 10:17 NIV

No giant will ever be a match for a big God with a little rock.

Beth Moore

MORE WORDS FROM GOD'S WORD

With God's power working in us, God can do much, much more than anything we can ask or imagine.

Ephesians 3:20 NCV

Proclaim the power of God, whose majesty is over Israel, whose power is in the skies. You are awesome, O God, in your sanctuary; the God of Israel gives power and strength to his people. Praise be to God!

Psalm 68:34-35 NIV

Ah, Lord God! Behold, You have made the heavens and the earth by Your great power and outstretched arm. There is nothing too hard for You.

Jeremiah 32:17 NKJV

My Priorities for Life

When I place my faith in God, life becomes a grand adventure.

Worship reminds me of the awesome power of God. I worship Him daily, and seek to allow Him to work through me.

I expect God to work miracles.

	Check Your Priority	
High	Med.	Low
—	—	—
—	—	—
—	—	—

Living Courageously

Be strong and courageous, and do the work.
*Don't be afraid or discouraged by the size of the task, for the L*ORD *God,*
my God, is with you. He will not fail you or forsake you.

1 Chronicles 28:20 NLT

A storm rose quickly on the Sea of Galilee, and the disciples were afraid. Although they had seen Jesus perform many miracles, although they had walked side by side with the Son of God, the disciples feared for their lives. So they turned to their Savior, and He calmed the waters and the wind.

Sometimes, we, like the disciples, feel threatened by the inevitable storms of life. When we are fearful, we, too, can turn to Christ for courage and for comfort. When we do so, He calms our fears just as surely as He calmed the winds and the waters two thousand years ago.

Billy Graham observed, "Down through the centuries, in times of trouble and trial, God has brought courage to the hearts of those who love Him. The Bible is filled with assurances of God's help and comfort in every kind of trouble which might cause fears to arise in the human heart. You can look ahead with promise, hope, and joy."

The next time you find your courage tested by the inevitable challenges of everyday living, remember that God is as near as your next breath. He is your shield and your strength; He is your protector and your deliverer. Call upon Him in your hour of need and then be comforted. Whatever your challenge, whatever your trouble, God can handle it. And will.

With each new experience of letting God be in control, we gain courage and reinforcement for daring to do it again and again.

Gloria Gaither

PRIORITIES FOR MY LIFE

Is your courage being tested? Cling tightly to God's promises, and pray. God can give you the strength to meet any challenge, and that's exactly what you should ask Him to do.

TIMELESS WISDOM FOR GODLY LIVING

Faith is stronger than fear.

John Maxwell

There comes a time when we simply have to face the challenges in our lives and stop backing down.

John Eldredge

Dreaming the dream of God is not for cowards.

Joey Johnson

What is courage? It is the ability to be strong in trust, in conviction, in obedience. To be courageous is to step out in faith— to trust and obey, no matter what.

Kay Arthur

*Therefore, being always of good courage . . .
we walk by faith, not by sight.*
2 Corinthians 5:6-7 NASB

God knows that the strength that comes from wrestling with our fear will give us wings to fly.

Paula Rinehart

MORE WORDS FROM GOD'S WORD

God doesn't want us to be shy with his gifts, but bold and loving and sensible.

2 Timothy 1:7 MSG

The LORD himself goes before you and will be with you; he will never leave you nor forsake you. Do not be afraid; do not be discouraged.

Deuteronomy 31:8 NIV

But Moses said to the people, "Do not fear! Stand by and see the salvation of the LORD.

Exodus 14:13 NASB

In thee, O Lord, do I put my trust; let me never be put into confusion.

Psalm 71:1 KJV

My Priorities for Life

	Check Your Priority		
	High	Med.	Low
I overcome fear by praying, and then by facing my fears head on.	—	—	—
I consider God to be my partner in every aspect of my life.	—	—	—
I understand the importance of living courageously.	—	—	—

Comforting Those in Need

*Blessed be the God and Father of our Lord Jesus Christ,
the Father of mercies and the God of all comfort. He comforts us
in all our affliction, so that we may be able to comfort those
who are in any kind of affliction, through the comfort
we ourselves receive from God.*

2 Corinthians 1:3-4 Holman CSB

Face it: we live in a world that is, on occasion, a frightening place. Sometimes, we sustain life-altering losses that are so profound and so tragic that it seems we could never recover. But, with God's help and with the help of encouraging family members and friends, we can recover.

In times of need, God's Word is clear: as believers, we must offer comfort to those in need by sharing not only our courage but also our faith. As the renowned revivalist Vance Havner observed, "No journey is complete that does not lead through some dark valleys. We can properly comfort others only with the comfort wherewith we ourselves have been comforted of God."

In times of adversity, we are wise to remember the words of Jesus, who, when He walked on the waters, reassured His disciples, saying, "Take courage! It is I. Don't be afraid" (Matthew 14:27 NIV). Then, with Christ on His throne—and with trusted

friends and loving family members at our sides—we can face our
fears with courage and with faith.

Discouraged people don't need critics.
They hurt enough already.
They don't need more guilt or piled-on distress.
They need encouragement.
They need a refuge, a willing, caring,
available someone.

Charles Swindoll

PRIORITIES FOR MY LIFE

Silence is okay. When you're offering comfort to a friend, your
presence may be more important than your words. Sometimes,
just being there is enough. If you're not sure what to say, don't.

TIMELESS WISDOM FOR GODLY LIVING

A Christian is someone who shares the sufferings of God in the world.

Dietrich Bonhoeffer

So often we think that to be encouragers we have to produce great words of wisdom when, in fact, a few simple syllables of sympathy and an arm around the shoulder can often provide much needed comfort.

Florence Littauer

> *Carry each other's burdens, and in this way*
> *you will fulfill the law of Christ.*
> Galatians 6:2 NIV

When we honestly ask ourselves which person in our lives means the most to us, we often find that it is he who, instead of giving much advice, solutions, and cures, has chosen rather to share our pain and touch our wounds with a gentle and tender hand. The friend who can be silent with us in a moment of despair or confusion, who can stay with us in an hour of grief and bereavement, who can tolerate not knowing, not curing, not healing, and face us with the reality of our powerlessness, that is a friend who cares.

Henri Nouwen

MORE WORDS FROM GOD'S WORD

Finally, all of you be of one mind, having compassion for one another; love as brothers, be tenderhearted, be courteous.

1 Peter 3:8 NKJV

So, as those who have been chosen of God, holy and beloved, put on a heart of compassion, kindness, humility, gentleness and patience.

Colossians 3:12 NASB

But he's already made it plain how to live, what to do, what God is looking for in men and women. It's quite simple: Do what is fair and just to your neighbor, be compassionate and loyal in your love, and don't take yourself too seriously—take God seriously.

Micah 6:8 MSG

My Priorities for Life

I understand the importance of offering comfort to my family and friends.

I believe that comforting others requires my presence and patience.

I believe that comforting others requires empathy and compassion.

Check Your Priority		
High	Med.	Low
—	—	—
—	—	—
—	—	—

The Rewards of Righteousness

For the eyes of the Lord are on the righteous,
and His ears are open to their prayers; but the face of the Lord
is against those who do evil.

1 Peter 3:12 NKJV

Do you want to be successful and happy? If so, here's a good place to start: Obey God. When you're faced with a difficult choice or a powerful temptation, pray about it. Invite God into your heart and live according to His commandments. When you do, you will be blessed today and tomorrow and forever.

Each new day presents countless opportunities to put God in first place . . . or not. When we honor Him by living according to His commandments, we earn for ourselves the abundance and peace that He promises. But, when we concern ourselves more with pleasing others than with pleasing our Creator, we bring needless suffering upon ourselves and our families. Would you like a time-tested formula for successful living? Here is a formula that is proven and true: Seek God's approval in every aspect of your life. Does this sound too simple? Perhaps it is simple, but it is also the only way to reap the marvelous riches that God has in store for you.

So today, take every step of your journey with God as your traveling companion. Read His Word and follow His commandments. Support only those activities that further God's kingdom and your own spiritual growth. Then, reap the blessings that God has promised to all those who live according to His will and His Word.

Let us never suppose that obedience is impossible
or that holiness is meant only for a select few.
Our Shepherd leads us in paths of righteousness—
not for our name's sake but for His.

Elisabeth Elliot

PRIORITIES FOR MY LIFE

Righteous living leads to joy. Bill Hybels observes, "Christianity says we were created by a righteous God to flourish and be exhilarated in a righteous environment. God has 'wired' us in such a way that the more righteous we are, the more we'll actually enjoy life." Holy living doesn't take the joy out of life; it puts it in.

TIMELESS WISDOM FOR GODLY LIVING

If we don't hunger and thirst after righteousness, we'll become anemic and feel miserable in our Christian experience.

Franklin Graham

We must appropriate the tender mercy of God every day after conversion, or problems quickly develop. We need his grace daily in order to live a righteous life.

Jim Cymbala

He doesn't need an abundance of words. He doesn't need a dissertation about your life. He just wants your attention. He wants your heart.

Kathy Troccoli

A man who lives right, and is right, has more power in his silence than another has by his words.

Phillips Brooks

Walk in a manner worthy of the God who calls you into His own kingdom and glory.
1 Thessalonians 2:12 NASB

Sanctify yourself and you will sanctify society.

St. Francis of Assisi

MORE WORDS FROM GOD'S WORD

Discipline yourself for the purpose of godliness.

1 Timothy 4:7 NASB

Run away from infantile indulgence. Run after mature righteousness— faith, love, peace—joining those who are in honest and serious prayer before God.

2 Timothy 2:22 MSG

And you shall do what is right and good in the sight of the Lord, that it may be well with you.

Deuteronomy 6:18 NKJV

The righteous shall flourish like the palm tree: he shall grow like a cedar in Lebanon.

Psalm 92:12 KJV

My Priorities for Life

I understand the importance of setting a good example for my family and friends.

I understand the value of living a life that is pleasing to God.

As my own example for living, I look to Jesus.

	Check Your Priority	
High	Med.	Low
—	—	—
—	—	—
—	—	—

Wisdom According to Whom?

*The Lord says, "I will make you wise and show you where to go.
I will guide you and watch over you."*

Psalm 32:8 NCV

Are you a wise guy (or girl)? And, are you becoming a little wiser every day? Hopefully so.

All of us would like to be wise, but not all of us are willing to do the work that is required to become wise. Why? Because wisdom isn't free—it takes time and effort to acquire.

To become wise, we must seek God's wisdom and live according to His Word. To become wise, we must seek wisdom with consistency and purpose. To become wise, we must not only learn the lessons of the Christian life; we must also live by them.

If you sincerely desire to become wise—and if you seek to share your hard-earned wisdom with others—your actions must give credence to your words. The best way to share one's wisdom—perhaps the only way—is not by words, but by example.

Wisdom is like a savings account: If you add to it consistently, then eventually you'll have a great sum. The secret to success is consistency. Do you seek wisdom? Then seek it every day, and seek it in the right place. That place, of course, is, first and foremost, the Word of God.

If we neglect the Bible, we cannot expect to benefit
from the wisdom and direction that result from
knowing God's Word.

Vonette Bright

The essence of wisdom, from a practical standpoint,
is pausing long enough to look at our lives—invitations,
opportunities, relationships—from God's perspective.
And then acting on it.

Charles Stanley

PRIORITIES FOR MY LIFE

Need wisdom? God's got it. If you want it, then study God's Word and associate with godly people.

TIMELESS WISDOM FOR GODLY LIVING

Wisdom enlarges our capacity for discovery and delight, causing wonder to grow as we grow.

Susan Lenzkes

Indeed, wisdom and discernment are among the natural results of a prayer-filled life.

Richard Foster

Knowledge can be learned, but wisdom must be earned. Wisdom is knowledge . . . lived.

Sheila Walsh

Wisdom is the principal thing; therefore get wisdom. And in all your getting, get understanding.
Proverbs 4:7 NKJV

Having a doctrine pass before the mind is not what the Bible means by knowing the truth. It's only when it reaches down deep into the heart that the truth begins to set us free, just as a key must penetrate a lock to turn it, or as rainfall must saturate the earth down to the roots in order for your garden to grow.

John Eldredge

MORE WORDS FROM GOD'S WORD

Anyone who listens to my teaching and obeys me is wise, like a person who builds a house on solid rock. Though the rain comes in torrents and the floodwaters rise and the winds beat against that house, it won't collapse, because it is built on rock.

Matthew 7:24–25 NLT

But the wisdom that is from above is first pure, then peaceable, gentle, willing to yield, full of mercy and good fruits, without partiality and without hypocrisy.

James 3:17 NKJV

The fear of the LORD is the beginning of wisdom, and knowledge of the Holy One is understanding.

Proverbs 9:10 NIV

My Priorities for Life

	Check Your Priority	
High	Med.	Low

I try to select friends who can help me become a better and wiser person.

— — —

I do my best to live wisely by obeying God's commandments.

— — —

I will continually remind myself of God's wisdom by reading the Bible each day.

— — —

A New Creation

His message was simple and austere, like his desert surroundings:
"Change your life. God's kingdom is here."

Matthew 3:2 MSG

If you're a Christian, here's a question you should ask yourself: Are you a different person because of your decision to form a personal relationship with Jesus? And while you're at it, here's another question: Does your relationship with Christ make a meaningful difference in the way that you live your life, or are you more or less the same person you might be if you were not a Christian? The answers to these questions will determine the level of your commitment to God and the direction of your life.

If you're still doing all the same things that non-believers do, it's time to take an honest look at the current condition of your faith. Why? Because Jesus doesn't want you to be a run-of-the-mill, follow-the-crowd kind of person. Jesus intends that you become a "new creation" through Him. And that's exactly what you should want for yourself, too.

Each new day presents countless opportunities to put God in first place, second place, or last place. Oswald Chambers noted, "If the Spirit of God has transformed you within, you will exhibit Divine characteristics in your life, not good human characteristics. God's life in us expresses itself as God's life, not as a human life trying to be godly."

When you invited Christ to reign over your heart, you became a radically new creation. This day offers yet another chance to behave yourself like that new person. When you do, God will guide your steps and bless your endeavors, beginning now and ending never.

In the midst of the pressure and the heat,
I am confident His hand is on my life,
developing my faith until I display His glory,
transforming me into a vessel of honor
that pleases Him!

Anne Graham Lotz

PRIORITIES FOR MY LIFE

The time is now: If you have already welcomed Christ into your heart as your personal Savior, then you are safe. If you're still sitting on the fence, the time to accept Him is this very moment.

TIMELESS WISDOM FOR GODLY LIVING

God's omniscience can instill you with a supernatural confidence that can transform your life.

Bill Hybels

God became man to turn creatures into sons: not simply to produce better men of the old kind but to produce a new kind of man.

C. S. Lewis

Believe and do what God says. The life-changing consequences will be limitless, and the results will be confidence and peace of mind.

Franklin Graham

God's work is not in buildings, but in transformed lives.

Ruth Bell Graham

Your old sinful self has died, and your new life is kept with Christ in God.

Colossians 3:3 NCV

For God is, indeed, a wonderful Father who longs to pour out His mercy upon us, and whose majesty is so great that He can transform us from deep within.

St. Teresa of Avila

MORE WORDS FROM GOD'S WORD

Therefore, brothers, by the mercies of God, I urge you to present your bodies as a living sacrifice, holy and pleasing to God; this is your spiritual worship. Do not be conformed to this age, but be transformed by the renewing of your mind, so that you may discern what is the good, pleasing, and perfect will of God.

Romans 12:1-2 Holman CSB

Your old life is dead. Your new life, which is your real life—even though invisible to spectators—is with Christ in God. He is your life.

Colossians 3:3 MSG

My Priorities for Life

I will ask God to give me the strength, the courage, and the wisdom to free myself from the chains that hold me back.

I will be willing to make major changes in my life if I believe that those changes will make me a better person.

I understand the importance of working to overcome the internal or external obstacles that keep me from becoming the person God wants me to be.

Check Your Priority		
High	Med.	Low
—	—	—
—	—	—
—	—	—

The Wisdom of Thanksgiving

In everything give thanks;
for this is the will of God in Christ Jesus for you.

1 Thessalonians 5:18 NKJV

Are you basically a thankful person? Do you appreciate the stuff you've got and the life that you're privileged to live? You most certainly should be thankful. After all, when you stop to think about it, God has given you more blessings than you can count. So the question of the day is this: will you slow down long enough to thank your Heavenly Father . . . or not?

Sometimes, life-here-on-earth can be complicated, demanding, and frustrating. When the demands of life leave you rushing from place to place with scarcely a moment to spare, you may fail to pause and thank your Creator for the countless blessings He has given you. Failing to thank God is understandable . . . but it's wrong.

God's Word makes it clear: a wise heart is a thankful heart. Period. Your Heavenly Father has blessed you beyond measure, and you owe Him everything, including your thanks. God is always listening—are you willing to say thanks? It's up to you, and the next move is yours.

Thanksgiving is good but Thanksliving is better.

Jim Gallery

My counsel for you is simple and straightforward:
Just go ahead with what you've been given. You received Christ Jesus,
the Master; now live him. You're deeply rooted in him.
You're well constructed upon him. You know your way around the faith.
Now do what you've been taught. School's out; quit studying the subject
and start living it! And let your living spill over into thanksgiving.

Colossians 2:6-7 MSG

PRIORITIES FOR MY LIFE

When is the best time to say "thanks" to God? Any Time. God loves you all the time, and that's exactly why you should praise Him all the time.

TIMELESS WISDOM FOR GODLY LIVING

If you can't tell whether your glass is half-empty or half-full, you don't need another glass; what you need is better eyesight . . . and a more thankful heart.

Marie T. Freeman

Thanksgiving invites God to bestow a second benefit.

Robert Herrick

The best way to show my gratitude to God is to accept everything, even my problems, with joy.

Mother Teresa

The act of thanksgiving is a demonstration of the fact that you are going to trust and believe God.

Kay Arthur

Our prayers for you are always spilling over into thanksgivings. We can't quit thanking God our Father and Jesus our Messiah for you!

Colossians 1:3 MSG

Grace and gratitude belong together like heaven and earth. Grace evokes gratitude like the voice of an echo. Gratitude follows grace as thunder follows lightning.

Karl Barth

MORE WORDS FROM GOD'S WORD

Finally, brethren, whatsoever things are true, whatsoever things are honest, whatsoever things are just, whatsoever things are pure, whatsoever things are lovely, whatsoever things are of good report; if there be any virtue, and if there be any praise, think on these things.

Philippians 4:8 KJV

Thanks be to God for His indescribable gift!

2 Corinthians 9:15 NKJV

I will thank you, Lord, with all my heart; I will tell of all the marvelous things you have done. I will be filled with joy because of you. I will sing praises to your name, O Most High.

Psalm 9:1-2 NLT

My Priorities for Life

I understand the importance of remaining humble as I praise God and thank Him for His gifts.

I understand that I should never take my blessings for granted.

I will not only thank God for His gifts; I will use those gifts as one way of honoring Him.

	Check Your Priority	
High	Med.	Low
—	—	—
—	—	—
—	—	—

Character Counts

Do not be misled: "Bad company corrupts good character."

1 Corinthians 15:33 NIV

It has been said that character is what we are when nobody is watching. How true. But, as Bill Hybels correctly observed, "Every secret act of character, conviction, and courage has been observed in living color by our omniscient God." And isn't that a sobering thought?

When we do things that we know aren't right, we try to hide our misdeeds from family members and friends. But even then, God is watching.

Living a life of integrity isn't always the easiest way, but it is always the right way. And God clearly intends that it should be your way, too. So if you find yourself tempted to break the truth—or even to bend it—remember that honesty is God's policy . . . and it must also be yours.

Simply put, if you sincerely want to walk with God, you must try, to the best of your ability, to follow His commandments. When you do, your character will take care of itself . . . and you won't need to look over your shoulder to see who, besides God, is watching.

Character is formed by doing the thing
we are supposed to do, when it should be done,
whether we feel like doing it or not.

Father Flanagan

There is something about having endured
great loss that brings purity of purpose
and strength of character.

Barbara Johnson

PRIORITIES FOR MY LIFE

One of your greatest possessions is integrity . . . don't lose it. Billy Graham was right when he said, "Integrity is the glue that holds our way of life together. We must constantly strive to keep our integrity intact. When wealth is lost, nothing is lost; when health is lost, something is lost; when character is lost, all is lost." And he's right!

TIMELESS WISDOM FOR GODLY LIVING

Character cannot be developed in ease and quiet. Only through experience of trial and suffering can the soul be strengthened, vision cleared, ambition inspired, and success achieved.

Helen Keller

Each one of us is God's special work of art. Through us, He teaches and inspires, delights and encourages, informs and uplifts all those who view our lives. God, the master artist, is most concerned about expressing Himself—His thoughts and His intentions—through what He paints in our characters.

Joni Eareckson Tada

Character is made in the small moments of our lives.

Phillips Brooks

Applying all diligence,
in your faith supply moral excellence.
2 Peter 1:5 NASB

Character is both developed and revealed by tests, and all of life is a test.

Rick Warren

MORE WORDS FROM GOD'S WORD

The righteousness of the blameless clears his path, but the wicked person will fall because of his wickedness.

Proverbs 11:5 Holman CSB

A good name is more desirable than great riches; to be esteemed is better than silver or gold.

Proverbs 22:1 NIV

We also have joy with our troubles, because we know that these troubles produce patience. And patience produces character, and character produces hope.

Romans 5:3-4 NCV

As in water face reflects face, so the heart of man reflects man.

Proverbs 27:19 NASB

My Priorities for Life

I understand that my power to witness for Christ depends upon my actions as well as my words.

I believe that character matters.

I try to do the right thing because I have to live with myself.

Check Your Priority		
High	Med.	Low
—	—	—
—	—	—
—	—	—

Putting Possessions in Proper Perspective

A pretentious, showy life is an empty life;
a plain and simple life is a full life.

Proverbs 13:7 MSG

Okay, be honest—are you in love with stuff? If so, you're headed for trouble, and fast. Why? Because no matter how much you love stuff, stuff won't love you back. In the life of committed Christian, material possessions should play a rather small role. Of course, we all need the basic necessities of life, but once we meet those needs for ourselves and for our families, the piling up of possessions creates more problems than it solves. Our real riches, of course, are not of this world. We are never really rich until we are rich in spirit.

Martin Luther observed, "Many things I have tried to grasp and have lost. That which I have placed in God's hands I still have." His words apply to all of us. Our earthly riches are transitory; our spiritual riches are not.

Do you find yourself wrapped up in the concerns of the material world? If so, it's time to reorder your priorities by turning your thoughts and your prayers to more important matters. And, it's time to begin storing up riches that will endure throughout eternity: the spiritual kind.

When we put people before possessions in our hearts, we are sowing seeds of enduring satisfaction.

Beverly LaHaye

Great wealth is not related to money! It is an attitude of satisfaction coupled with inner peace.

Charles Swindoll

PRIORITIES FOR MY LIFE

Stuff 101: The world says, "Buy more stuff." God says, "Stuff isn't important." Believe God.

TIMELESS WISDOM FOR GODLY LIVING

I have held many things in my hands, and I have lost them all; but whatever I have placed in God's hands, that I still possess.

Corrie ten Boom

He is no fool who gives what he cannot keep to gain what he cannot lose.

Jim Elliot

God may be in the process of pruning something out of your life at this very moment. If this is the case, don't fight it. Instead, welcome it, for His pruning will make you more fruitful and bring greater glory to the Father.

Rick Yohn

> *We brought nothing into the world,*
> *so we can take nothing out. But, if we have food*
> *and clothes, we will be satisfied with that.*
> 1 Timothy 6:7-8 NCV

Money, self-righteousness, religious works—all of these are cheap substitutes for the true riches we have in Jesus Christ.

Warren Wiersbe

MORE WORDS FROM GOD'S WORD

Your heart will be where your treasure is.

Luke 12:34 NCV

Can your wealth or all [your] physical exertion keep [you] from distress?

Job 36:19 Holman CSB

For what will it profit a man if he gains the whole world, and loses his own soul? Or what will a man give in exchange for his soul?

Mark 8:36-37 NKJV

Do not love the world or the things in the world. If anyone loves the world, the love of the Father is not in him.

1 John 2:15 NKJV

My Priorities for Life

I believe it is important to place spiritual possessions above material ones.

I believe that my enjoyment of life has less to do with material possessions and more to do with my relationships—beginning with my relationship to God.

Every day I will work to make certain that my possessions don't possess me.

Check Your Priority		
High	Med.	Low
—	—	—
—	—	—
—	—	—

Discovering His Peace

I leave you peace; my peace I give you.
I do not give it to you as the world does.
So don't let your hearts be troubled or afraid.

John 14:27 NCV

Oftentimes, our outer struggles are simply manifestations of the inner conflict that we feel when we stray from God's path.

Have you found the genuine peace that can be yours through Jesus Christ? Or are you still rushing after the illusion of "peace and happiness" that the world promises but cannot deliver? The beautiful words of John 14:27 remind us that Jesus offers us peace, not as the world gives, but as He alone gives. Your challenge is to accept Christ's peace and to share it with your friends and neighbors.

Today, as a gift to yourself, to your family, and to your friends, claim the inner peace that is your spiritual birthright: the peace of Jesus Christ. It is offered freely; it has been paid for in full; it is yours for the asking. So ask. And then share.

For Jesus peace seems to have meant
not the absence of struggle
but the presence of love.

Frederick Buechner

*And the peace of God, which surpasses all understanding,
will guard your hearts and minds through Christ Jesus. Finally, brethren,
whatever things are true, whatever things are noble, whatever things
are just, whatever things are pure, whatever things are lovely,
whatever things are of good report, if there is any virtue and
if there is anything praiseworthy—meditate on these things.*

Philippians 4:7-8 NKJV

PRIORITIES FOR MY LIFE

Sometimes peace is a scarce commodity in a demanding, 21st-century world. How can we find the peace that we so desperately desire? By turning our days and our lives over to God. May we give our lives, our hopes, and our prayers to the Father, and, by doing so, accept His will and His peace.

TIMELESS WISDOM FOR GODLY LIVING

There may be no trumpet sound or loud applause when we make a right decision, just a calm sense of resolution and peace.

Gloria Gaither

Where the soul is full of peace and joy, outward surroundings and circumstances are of comparatively little account.

Hannah Whitall Smiith

We need to be at peace with our past, content with our present, and sure about our future, knowing they are all in God's hands.

Joyce Meyer

What peace can they have who are not at peace with God?

Matthew Henry

If your sinful nature controls your mind, there is death. But if the Holy Spirit controls your mind, there is life and peace.

Romans 8:6 NLT

God is in control of history; it's His story. Doesn't that give you a great peace—especially when world events seems so tumultuous and insane?

Kay Arthur

MORE WORDS FROM GOD'S WORD

If it is possible, as far as it depends on you, live at peace with everyone.

Romans 12:18 NIV

Blessed are the peacemakers, for they will be called sons of God.

Matthew 5:9 NIV

Live peaceful and quiet lives in all godliness and holiness.

1 Timothy 2:2 NIV

You, Lord, give true peace to those who depend on you, because they trust you.

Isaiah 26:3 NCV

My Priorities for Life

	Check Your Priority	
High	Med.	Low

I understand the importance of living a peaceful life.

  —   —   —

I find that the more time I spend in prayer, the more peaceful I feel.

  —   —   —

I trust that God can give me a peace that passes my understanding.

  —   —   —

And the Greatest
of These . . .

Though I speak with the tongues of men and of angels, but have not love,
I have become sounding brass or a clanging cymbal.

1 Corinthians 13:1 NKJV

Love, like everything else in this wonderful world, begins
and ends with God, but the middle part belongs to us.
During the brief time that we have here on earth, God has
given each of us the opportunity to become a loving person—or
not. God has given each of us the opportunity to be kind, to be
courteous, to be cooperative, and to be forgiving—or not. God
has given each of us the chance to obey the Golden Rule, or to
make up our own rules as we go. If we obey God's rules, we're
safe, but if we do otherwise, we're headed for trouble in a hurry.

There's an old saying that's both trite and true: If you aren't
loving, you aren't living. But here in the real world, it isn't always
easy to love other people, especially when those people have done
things to hurt you. Still, God's Word is clear: you are instructed
to love others despite their imperfections.

God does not intend for you to experience mediocre
relationships; He created you for far greater things. Building
lasting relationships requires compassion, wisdom, empathy,
kindness, courtesy, and forgiveness. If that sounds a lot like work,

it is—which is perfectly fine with God. Why? Because He knows that you are capable of doing that work, and because He knows that the fruits of your labors will enrich the lives of your loved ones and the lives of generations yet unborn.

> Each year some new heart finally hears,
> finally sees, finally knows love,
> and in heaven, there is great rejoicing!
> The Child is born anew,
> and one more knee is bowed!

Ann Weems

PRIORITIES FOR MY LIFE

Beware! Love at first sight always deserves a second look. If you give your heart away too easily or too often, you may find that it is returned to you . . . in very poor condition!

TIMELESS WISDOM FOR GODLY LIVING

Only God can give us a selfless love for others, as the Holy Spirit changes us from within.

Billy Graham

Love is something like the clouds that were in the sky before the sun came out. You cannot touch the clouds, you know; but you feel the rain and know how glad the flowers and the thirsty earth are to have it after a hot day. You cannot touch love either; but you feel the sweetness that it pours into everything.

Annie Sullivan

Love is a far better stimulus than threat or pressure.

Brennan Manning

We long to find someone who has been where we've been, who shares our fragile skies, who sees our sunsets with the same shades of blue.

Beth Moore

> *Beloved, if God so loved us,*
> *we also ought to love one another.*
> 1 John 4:11 NASB

How much a person loves someone is obvious by how much he is willing to sacrifice for that person.

Bill Bright

MORE WORDS FROM GOD'S WORD

Love one another deeply, from the heart.

1 Peter 1:22 NIV

May the Lord cause you to increase and abound in love for one another, and for all people.

1 Thessalonians 3:12 NASB

Now these three remain: faith, hope, and love. But the greatest of these is love.

1 Corinthians 13:13 Holman CSB

My Priorities for Life

When I have been hurt by someone, I understand the importance of forgiving that person as quickly as possible and as completely as possible.

Because I place a high priority on my relationships, I am willing to invest the time and energy that is required to make those relationships work.

As a follower of Christ, I understand that I am commanded to love other people, and I take that commandment seriously.

Check Your Priority		
High	Med.	Low
—	—	—
—	—	—
—	—	—

The Choice to Rejoice

Let the hearts of those who seek the Lord rejoice.
Look to the Lord and his strength; seek his face always.

1 Chronicles 16:10-11 NIV

Have you made the choice to rejoice? If you're a Christian, you have every reason to be joyful. After all, the ultimate battle has already been won on the cross at Calvary. And if your life has been transformed by Christ's sacrifice, then you, as a recipient of God's grace, have every reason to live joyfully. Yet sometimes, amid the inevitable hustle and bustle of life-here-on-earth, you may lose sight of your blessings as you wrestle with the challenges of everyday life.

Do you want to be a happy, contented person? If so, here are some things you should do: Love God and His Son; depend upon God for strength; try, to the best of your abilities, to follow God's will; and strive to obey His Holy Word. When you do these things, you'll discover that happiness goes hand-in-hand with righteousness. The happiest people are not those who rebel against God; the happiest people are those who love God and obey His commandments.

What does life have in store for you? A world full of possibilities (of course it's up to you to seize them), and God's promise of abundance (of course it's up to you to accept it). So, as you embark upon the next phase of your journey, remember to celebrate the life that God has given you. Your Creator has blessed you beyond measure. Honor Him with your prayers, your words, your deeds, and your joy.

Joy is the serious business of heaven.

C. S. Lewis

According to Jesus, it is God's will that His children be filled with the joy of life.

Catherine Marshall

PRIORITIES FOR MY LIFE

Joy begins with a choice—the choice to establish a genuine relationship with God and His Son. As Amy Carmichael correctly observed, "Joy is not gush; joy is not mere jolliness. Joy is perfect acquiescence, acceptance, and rest in God's will, whatever comes."

TIMELESS WISDOM FOR GODLY LIVING

Joy has nothing to do with circumstances. Joy is a choice. It is a matter of attitude that stems from one's confidence in God.

Charles Swindoll

Jesus did not promise to change the circumstances around us. He promised great peace and pure joy to those who would learn to believe that God actually controls all things.

Corrie ten Boom

True happiness and contentment cannot come from the things of this world. The blessedness of true joy is a free gift that comes only from our Lord and Savior, Jesus Christ.

Dennis Swanberg

*Rejoice evermore. Pray without ceasing.
In every thing give thanks: for this is the will of God
in Christ Jesus concerning you.*
1 Thessalonians 5:16-18 KJV

Among the most joyful people I have known have been some who seem to have had no human reason for joy. The sweet fragrance of Christ has shown through their lives.

Elisabeth Elliot

MORE WORDS FROM GOD'S WORD

These things I have spoken to you, that My joy may remain in you, and that your joy may be full.

John 15:11 NKJV

Always be full of joy in the Lord. I say it again—rejoice!

Philippians 4:4 NLT

Rejoice, and be exceeding glad: for great is your reward in heaven . . . .

Matthew 5:12 KJV

Shout for joy to the LORD, all the earth. Worship the LORD with gladness; come before him with joyful songs.

Psalm 100:1-2 NIV

My Priorities for Life

	Check Your Priority	
High	Med.	Low

I strive to worry less and trust God more.

— — —

I do what I can to share my enthusiasm with family, with friends, and with the world.

— — —

I do my best to treat each day of my life as a cause for celebration.

— — —

I praise God many times each day.

— — —

The Rule That Is Golden

Let us not become weary in doing good,
for at the proper time we will reap a harvest if we do not give up.

Galatians 6:9 NIV

Is the Golden Rule your rule, or is it just another Bible verse that goes in one ear and out the other? Jesus made Himself perfectly clear: He instructed you to treat other people in the same way that you want to be treated. But sometimes, especially when you're feeling pressure from friends, or when you're tired or upset, obeying the Golden Rule can seem like an impossible task—but it's not.

God wants each of us to treat other people with respect, kindness, and courtesy. He wants us to rise above our own imperfections, and He wants us to treat others with unselfishness and love. To make it short and sweet, God wants us to obey the Golden Rule, and He knows we can do it.

So if you're wondering how to treat someone else, ask the person you see every time you look into the mirror. The answer you receive will tell you exactly what to do.

It is one of the most beautiful compensations
of life that no one can sincerely try to
help another without helping herself.

Barbara Johnson

Carry each other's burdens,
and in this way you will fulfill the law of Christ.

Galatians 6:2 NIV

PRIORITIES FOR MY LIFE

When you're trying to decide how to treat another person, ask
yourself this question: "How would I feel if somebody treated me
that way?" Then, treat the other person the way that you would
want to be treated.

TIMELESS WISDOM FOR GODLY LIVING

Anything done for another is done for oneself.

Pope John Paul II

It is wrong for anyone to be anxious to receive more from his neighbor than he himself is willing to give to God.

St. Francis of Assisi

The Golden Rule starts at home, but it should never stop there.

Marie T. Freeman

We should behave to our friends as we would wish our friends to behave to us.

Aristotle

Each of you should look not only to your own interests, but also to the interest of others.
Philippians 2:4 NIV

Here lies the tremendous mystery—that God should be all-powerful, yet refuse to coerce. He summons us to cooperation. We are honored in being given the opportunity to participate in His good deeds. Remember how He asked for help in performing His miracles: Fill the water pots, stretch out your hand, distribute the loaves.

Elisabeth Elliot

MORE WORDS FROM GOD'S WORD

So in everything, do to others what you would have them do to you, for this sums up the Law and the Prophets.

Matthew 7:12 NIV

Give to everyone who asks you, and if anyone takes what belongs to you, do not demand it back.

Luke 6:30 NIV

Let us not become weary in doing good, for at the proper time we will reap a harvest if we do not give up.

Galatians 6:9 NIV

See that no one renders evil for evil to anyone, but always pursue what is good both for yourselves and for all.

1 Thessalonians 5:15 NKJV

My Priorities for Life

	Check Your Priority		
	High	Med.	Low
When dealing with other people, I believe that it is important to try to "walk in their shoes."	—	—	—
I believe that it is important to treat all people with respect and kindness.	—	—	—
I find that when I treat others with respect, I feel better about myself.	—	—	—

God's Perfect Love

We know how much God loves us,
and we have put our trust in him. God is love,
and all who live in love live in God, and God lives in them.

1 John 4:16 NLT

How much does God love you? As long as you're alive, you'll never be able to figure it out because God's love is just too big to comprehend. But this much we know: God loves you so much that He sent His Son Jesus to come to this earth and to die for you! And, when you accepted Jesus into your heart, God gave you a gift that is more precious than gold: the gift of eternal life.

Sometimes, in the crush of your daily activities, God may seem far away, but He is not. God is with you night and day; He knows your thoughts and your prayers. And, when you earnestly seek Him, you will find Him because He is here, waiting patiently for you to reach out to Him.

St. Augustine observed, "God loves each of us as if there were only one of us." Do you believe those words? Do you seek to have an intimate, one-on-one relationship with your Heavenly Father, or are you satisfied to keep Him at a "safe" distance?

God's love is bigger and more powerful than anybody can imagine, but His love is very real. So do yourself a favor right now: accept God's love with open arms and welcome His Son Jesus into your heart. When you do, your life will be changed today, tomorrow, and forever.

If God had a refrigerator, your picture would be on it.
If he had a wallet, your photo would be in it.
He sends you flowers every spring and a sunrise every morning.

Max Lucado

God will never let you be shaken or moved
from your place near His heart.

Joni Eareckson Tada

PRIORITIES FOR MY LIFE

Remember: God's love for you is too big to understand with your brain . . . but it's not too big to feel with your heart.

TIMELESS WISDOM FOR GODLY LIVING

. . . God loves these people too, just because they're unattractive or warped in their thinking doesn't mean the Lord doesn't love them.

Ruth Bell Graham

God knows all that is true about us and is a friend to the face we show and the face we hide. He does not love us less for our human weaknesses.

Sheila Walsh

Joy comes from knowing God loves me and knows who I am and where I'm going . . . that my future is secure as I rest in Him.

James Dobson

As the Father loved Me,
I also have loved you; abide in My love.
John 15:9 NKJV

The hope we have in Jesus is the anchor for the soul—something sure and steadfast, preventing drifting or giving way, lowered to the depth of God's love.

Franklin Graham

MORE WORDS FROM GOD'S WORD

For God so loved the world, that he gave his only begotten Son, that whosoever believeth in him should not perish, but have everlasting life.

John 3:16 KJV

The unfailing love of the LORD never ends! By his mercies we have been kept from complete destruction.

Lamentations 3:22 NLT

His banner over me was love.

Song of Solomon 2:4 KJV

But God demonstrates His own love toward us, in that while we were still sinners, Christ died for us.

Romans 5:8 NKJV

My Priorities for Life

| | Check Your Priority | |
High	Med.	Low

I understand the importance of sharing God's love with my family and friends.

— — —

I understand the importance of having a loving relationship with God by spending time with Him.

— — —

I believe that God loves me.

— — —

Following Christ

Then he told them what they could expect for themselves:
"Anyone who intends to come with me has to let me lead."

Luke 9:23 MSG

Who are you going to walk with today? Are you going to walk with people who worship the ways of the world? Or are you going to walk with the Son of God? Jesus walks with you. Are you walking with Him? Hopefully, you will choose to walk with Him today and every day of your life.

Jesus loved you so much that He endured unspeakable humiliation and suffering for you. How will you respond to Christ's sacrifice? Will you take up His cross and follow Him (Luke 9:23), or will you choose another path? When you place your hopes squarely at the foot of the cross, when you place Jesus squarely at the center of your life, you will be blessed.

The 19th-century writer Hannah Whitall Smith observed, "The crucial question for each of us is this: What do you think of Jesus, and do you yet have a personal acquaintance with Him?" Indeed, the answer to that question determines the quality, the course, and the direction of our lives today and for all eternity.

Today provides another glorious opportunity to place yourself in the service of the One from Galilee. May you seek His will, may you trust His word, and may you walk in His footsteps— now and forever—amen.

Walk in the daylight of God's will because then you will be safe; you will not stumble.

Anne Graham Lotz

Whoever is not willing to carry the cross and follow me is not worthy of me. Those who try to hold on to their lives will give up true life. Those who give up their lives for me will hold on to true life.

Matthew 10:38-39 NCV

PRIORITIES FOR MY LIFE

If you want to be a little more like Christ . . . learn about His teachings, follow in His footsteps, and obey His commandments.

TIMELESS WISDOM FOR GODLY LIVING

When we truly walk with God throughout our day, life slowly starts to fall into place.

Bill Hybels

To walk out of His will is to walk into nowhere.

C. S. Lewis

Think of this—we may live together with Him here and now, a daily walking with Him who loved us and gave Himself for us.

Elisabeth Elliot

A disciple is a follower of Christ. That means you take on His priorities as your own. His agenda becomes your agenda. His mission becomes your mission.

Charles Stanley

I've laid down a pattern for you. What I've done, you do.
John 13:15 MSG

Imagine the spiritual strength the disciples drew from walking hundreds of miles with Jesus . . . (3 John 4).

Jim Maxwell

MORE WORDS FROM GOD'S WORD

No one can serve two masters. Either he will hate the one and love the other, or he will be devoted to the one and despise the other.

Matthew 6:24 NIV

Follow Me, Jesus told them, "and I will make you into fishers of men!" Immediately they left their nets and followed Him.

Mark 1:17-18 Holman CSB

You did not choose Me, but I chose you. I appointed you that you should go out and produce fruit, and that your fruit should remain, so that whatever you ask the Father in My name, He will give you.

John 15:16 Holman CSB

My Priorities for Life

I believe there is a joyful abundance that is mine when I follow Christ.

I believe that it is important for me to attempt to follow in Christ's footsteps, despite my imperfections.

I believe that my relationship with Jesus should be one of servant and Master. I am the servant and He is the Master.

Check Your Priority		
High	Med.	Low
—	—	—
—	—	—
—	—	—

The Power of Encouragement

So encourage each other and give each other strength,
just as you are doing now.

1 Thessalonians 5:11 NCV

Life is a team sport, and all of us need occasional pats on the back from our teammates. This world can be a difficult place, a place where many of our friends and family members are troubled by the challenges of everyday life. And since we cannot always be certain who needs our help, we should strive to speak helpful words to all who cross our paths.

Genuine encouragement should never be confused with pity. God intends for His children to lead lives of abundance, joy, celebration, and praise—not lives of self-pity or regret. So we must guard ourselves against hosting (or joining) the "pity parties" that so often accompany difficult times. Instead, we must encourage each other to have faith—first in God and His only begotten Son—and then in our own abilities to use the talents God has given us for the furtherance of His kingdom and for the betterment of our own lives.

As a faithful follower of Jesus, you have every reason to be hopeful, and you have every reason to share your hopes with others. When you do, you will discover that hope, like other human emotions, is contagious. So do the world (and yourself) a favor: Look for the good in others and celebrate the good that you find. When you do, you'll be a powerful force of encouragement to your friends and family . . . and a worthy servant to your God.

Words. Do you fully understand their power? Can any of us really grasp the mighty force behind the things we say? Do we stop and think before we speak, considering the potency of the words we utter?

Joni Eareckson Tada

PRIORITIES FOR MY LIFE

Sometimes, even a few words can make a very big difference. As Fanny Crosby observed, "A single word, if spoken in a friendly spirit, may be sufficient to turn one from dangerous error."

TIMELESS WISDOM FOR GODLY LIVING

To the loved, a word of affection is a morsel, but to the love-starved, a word of affection can be a feast.

Max Lucado

Encouragement is the oxygen of the soul.

John Maxwell

Giving encouragement to others is a most welcome gift, for the results of it are lifted spirits, increased self-worth, and a hopeful future.

Florence Littauer

We urgently need people who encourage and inspire us to move toward God and away from the world's enticing pleasures.

Jim Cymbala

He comes alongside us when we go through hard times, and before you know it, he brings us alongside someone else who is going through hard times so that we can be there for that person just as God was there for us.
2 Corinthians 1:4 MSG

I'd rather see a sermon than hear one any day; I'd rather one should walk with me than merely tell the way.

Edgar A. Guest

MORE WORDS FROM GOD'S WORD

Watch the way you talk. Let nothing foul or dirty come out of your mouth. Say only what helps, each word a gift.

Ephesians 4:29 MSG

Let the word of Christ dwell in you richly in all wisdom; teaching and admonishing one another in psalms and hymns and spiritual songs, singing with grace in your hearts to the Lord.

Colossians 3:16 KJV

But encourage one another day after day, as long as it is still called "Today," so that none of you will be hardened by the deceitfulness of sin.

Hebrews 3:13 NASB

My Priorities for Life

I understand that my words reflect my heart. I will guard my heart so that my words will be pleasing to God.

I carefully think about the words I speak so that every word might be a "gift of encouragement" to others.

I believe that God wants me to encourage other people.

Check Your Priority		
High	Med.	Low
—	—	—
—	—	—
—	—	—

Valuing Your Gifts

God has given gifts to each of you from his great variety of spiritual gifts. Manage them well so that God's generosity can flow through you.

1 Peter 4:10 NLT

God knew precisely what He was doing when He gave you a unique set of talents and opportunities. And now, God wants you to use those talents for the glory of His kingdom. So here's the big question: will you choose to use those talents, or not?

Your Heavenly Father wants you to be a faithful steward of the gifts He has given you. But you live in a society that may encourage you to do otherwise. You face countless temptations to squander your time, your resources, and your talents. So you must be keenly aware of the inevitable distractions that can waste your time, your energy, and your opportunities.

Every day of your life, you have a choice to make: to nurture your talents or neglect them. When you choose wisely, God rewards your efforts, and He expands your opportunities to serve Him.

God has blessed you with unique opportunities to serve Him, and He has given you every tool that you need to do so. Today, accept this challenge: value the talent that God has given you, nourish it, make it grow, and share it with the world. After all, the best way to say "Thank You" for God's gifts is to use them.

Not everyone possesses boundless energy or a conspicuous talent. We are not equally blessed with great intellect or physical beauty or emotional strength. But we have all been given the same ability to be faithful.

Gigi Graham Tchividjian

PRIORITIES FOR MY LIFE

Polishing your skills requires effort: Converting raw talent into polished skill usually requires work, and lots of it. God's Word clearly instructs you to do the hard work of refining your talents for the glory of His kingdom and the service of His people. So, we are wise to remember the old adage: "What you are is God's gift to you; what you become is your gift to God." And it's up to you to make sure that your gift is worthy of the Giver.

TIMELESS WISDOM FOR GODLY LIVING

God has given you special talents—now it's your turn to give them back to God.

Marie T. Freeman

If you want to reach your potential, you need to add a strong work ethic to your talent.

John Maxwell

God often reveals His direction for our lives through the way He made us . . . with a certain personality and unique skills.

Bill Hybels

You are the only person on earth who can use your ability.

Zig Ziglar

> *Do not neglect the gift that is in you.*
> *1 Timothy 4:14 Holman CSB*

In the great orchestra we call life, you have an instrument and a song, and you owe it to God to play them both sublimely.

Max Lucado

MORE WORDS FROM GOD'S WORD

I remind you to fan into flame the gift of God.

2 Timothy 1:6 NIV

There are different kinds of gifts, but they are all from the same Spirit. There are different ways to serve but the same Lord to serve.

1 Corinthians 12:4–5 NCV

We have different gifts, according to the grace given us. If a man's gift is prophesying, let him use it in proportion to his faith. If it is serving, let him serve; if it is teaching, let him teach; if it is encouraging, let him encourage; if it is contributing to the needs of others, let him give generously; if it is leadership, let him govern diligently; if it is showing mercy, let him do it cheerfully.

Romans 12:6-8 NIV

My Priorities for Life

	Check Your Priority		
	High	Med.	Low
I believe that it is important to associate with people who encourage me to use my talents.	—	—	—
I believe that God wants me to take risks to do the work that He intends for me to do.	—	—	—
I believe that it is important to honor God by using the talents He has given me.	—	—	—

A Lifetime of Learning

The fear of the Lord is the beginning of knowledge,
but fools despise wisdom and discipline.

Proverbs 1:7 NIV

Whether you're 19 or 119, you've still got lots to learn. Even if you're very wise, God isn't finished with you yet, and He isn't finished teaching you important lessons about life here on earth and life eternal.

God does not intend for you to be a stagnant believer. Far from it! God wants you to continue growing as a person and as a Christian every day that you live. And make no mistake: both spiritual and intellectual growth are possible during every stage of life.

Are you a curious Christian who has committed yourself to the regimen of regular Bible study, or do you consult your Bible on a hit-or-miss basis? The answer to this question will be an indication of the extent to which you allow God to direct the course of your life.

As a spiritual being, you have the potential to grow in your personal knowledge of the Lord every day that you live. You can do so through prayer, through worship, through an openness to God's Holy Spirit, and through a careful study of God's Holy

Word. Your Bible contains powerful prescriptions for everyday living. If you sincerely seek to walk with God, you should commit yourself to the thoughtful study of His teachings.

Do you seek to live a life of righteousness and wisdom? If so, you must continue to study the ultimate source of wisdom: the Word of God. You must associate, day in and day out, with godly men and women. And, you must act in accordance with your beliefs.

When you study God's Word and live according to His commandments, you will become wise . . . and you will serve as a shining example to your friends, to your family, and to the world.

Knowledge is power.

Francis Bacon

PRIORITIES FOR MY LIFE

Never stop learning. Think of it like this: when you're through learning, you're through.

TIMELESS WISDOM FOR GODLY LIVING

The man who never reads will never be read; he who never quotes will never be quoted. He who will not use the thoughts of other men's brains proves that he has no brains of his own.

C. H. Spurgeon

A big difference exists between a head full of knowledge and the words of God literally abiding in us.

Beth Moore

To know the will of God is the greatest knowledge! To do the will of God is the greatest achievement.

George W. Truett

An investment in knowledge always pays the best interest.

Ben Franklin

The knowledge of the secrets of the kingdom of heaven has been given to you . . . .
Matthew 13:11 NIV

Knowledge is power; knowledge is safety; knowledge is happiness.

George Washington Carver

MORE WORDS FROM GOD'S WORD

Knowing God leads to self-control. Self-control leads to patient endurance, and patient endurance leads to godliness.

2 Peter 1:6 NLT

Remember what you are taught, and listen carefully to words of knowledge.

Proverbs 23:12 NCV

It is not good to have zeal without knowledge, nor to be hasty and miss the way.

Proverbs 19:2 NIV

For now we see indistinctly, as in a mirror, but then face to face. Now I know in part, but then I will know fully, as I am fully known.

1 Corinthians 13:12 Holman CSB

My Priorities for Life

	Check Your Priority	
High	Med.	Low

God's wisdom sometimes opposes the world's wisdom; I choose God's wisdom.

— — —

I value the importance of learning.

— — —

I can learn from the past, but I don't choose to live in the past.

— — —

Tackling Tough Times

We also have joy with our troubles, because we know that these troubles produce patience. And patience produces character, and character produces hope.

Romans 5:3-4 NCV

The Bible promises this: tough times are temporary but God's love is not—God's love lasts forever. So what does that mean to you? Just this: From time to time, everybody faces tough times, and so will you. And when tough times arrive, God will always stand ready to protect you and heal you.

Psalm 147 promises, "He heals the brokenhearted" (v. 3, NIV), but Psalm 147 doesn't say that He heals them instantly. Usually, it takes time (and maybe even a little help from you) for God to fix things. So if you're facing tough times, face them with God by your side. If you find yourself in any kind of trouble, pray about it and ask God for help. And be patient. God will work things out, just as He has promised, but He will do it in His own way and in His own time.

As believers, we know that God loves us and that He will protect us. In times of hardship, He will comfort us; in times of sorrow, He will dry our tears. When we are troubled or weak or sorrowful, God is always with us. We must build our lives on the rock that cannot be shaken: we must trust in God. And then, we must get on with the hard work of tackling our problems . . . because if we don't, who will? Or should?

When you accept the fact that sometimes seasons are dry and times are hard and that God is in control of both, you will discover a sense of divine refuge because the hope then is in God and not in yourself.

Charles Swindoll

For though a righteous man falls seven times, he rises again . . . .

Proverbs 24:16 NIV

PRIORITIES FOR MY LIFE

Going through tough times? Maybe there's a lesson in there somewhere. If you're going through difficult times, consider it an opportunity for spiritual growth. And ask yourself this question: "What is God trying to teach me today?"

TIMELESS WISDOM FOR GODLY LIVING

When God allows extraordinary trials for His people, He prepares extraordinary comforts for them.

Corrie ten Boom

We can stand affliction better than we can stand prosperity, for in prosperity we forget God.

D. L. Moody

Life will be made or broken at the place where we meet and deal with obstacles.

E. Stanley Jones

God's curriculum for all who sincerely want to know Him and do His will always includes lessons we wish we could skip. With an intimate understanding of our deepest needs and individual capacities, He chooses our curriculum.

Elisabeth Elliot

> *The LORD also will be a stronghold for the oppressed,*
> *a stronghold in times of trouble.*
> *Psalm 9:9 NASB*

One sees great things from the valley; only small things from the peak.

G. K. Chesterton

MORE WORDS FROM GOD'S WORD

You pulled me from the brink of death, my feet from the cliff-edge of doom. Now I stroll at leisure with God in the sunlit fields of life.

Psalm 56:13 MSG

Don't fret or worry, Instead of worrying, pray. Let petitions and praises shape your worries into prayers, letting God know your concerns. Before you know it, a sense of God's wholeness, everything coming together for good, will come and settle you down. It's wonderful what happens when Christ displaces worry at the center of your life.

Philippians 4:6-7 MSG

The Lord lifts the burdens of those bent beneath their loads. The Lord loves the righteous.

Psalm 146:8 NLT

My Priorities for Life

	Check Your Priority	
High	Med.	Low

I understand the importance of comforting others who find themselves in difficult circumstances.

— — —

I believe that difficult times can also be times of intense personal growth.

— — —

In dealing with difficult situations, I view God as my comfort and my strength.

— — —

Above and Beyond Our Worries

So do not worry, saying, "What shall we eat?" or "What shall we drink?" or "What shall we wear?" For the pagans run after all these things, and your heavenly Father knows that you need them. But seek first his kingdom and his righteousness, and all these things will be given to you as well. Therefore do not worry about tomorrow, for tomorrow will worry about itself. Each day has enough trouble of its own.

Matthew 6:31-34 NIV

Because you have the ability to think, you also have the ability to worry. Even if you're a very faithful Christian, you may be plagued by occasional periods of discouragement and doubt. Even though you trust God's promise of salvation—even though you sincerely believe in God's love and protection—you may find yourself upset by the countless details of everyday life. When you're worried, there are two places you should take your concerns: to the people who love you and to God.

When troubles arise, it helps to talk about them with parents, concerned adults, and trusted friends. But you shouldn't stop there: you should also talk to God through your prayers.

If you're worried about something, pray about it. Remember that God is always listening, and He always wants to hear from you.

So when you're upset about something, try this simple plan: talk and pray. Talk openly to the people who love you, and pray to the Heavenly Father who made you. The more you talk and the more you pray, the better you'll feel.

> With the peace of God to guard us and the God of peace to guide us— why worry?
>
> *Warren Wiersbe*

PRIORITIES FOR MY LIFE

When you're having hard times, remember that this, too, will pass. And remember that it will pass more quickly if you spend more time solving problems and less time fretting over them.

TIMELESS WISDOM FOR GODLY LIVING

The closer you live to God, the smaller everything else appears.

Rick Warren

Never yield to gloomy anticipation. Place your hope and confidence in God. He has no record of failure.

Mrs. Charles E. Cowman

Worry makes you forget who's in charge.

Max Lucado

Since the Lord is your shepherd, what are you worried about?

Marie T. Freeman

Come to Me, all you who labor and are heavy laden, and I will give you rest. Take My yoke upon you and learn from Me, for I am gentle and lowly in heart, and you will find rest for your souls. For My yoke is easy and My burden is light.
Matthew 11:28-30 NKJV

Submit each day to God, knowing that He is God over all your tomorrows.

Kay Arthur

MORE WORDS FROM GOD'S WORD

I was very worried, but you comforted me . . . .

Psalm 94:19 NCV

Don't fret or worry, Instead of worrying, pray. Let petitions and praises shape your worries into prayers, letting God know your concerns. Before you know it, a sense of God's wholeness, everything coming together for good, will come and settle you down. It's wonderful what happens when Christ displaces worry at the center of your life.

Philippians 4:6-7 MSG

I will be with you when you pass through the waters . . . when you walk through the fire . . . the flame will not burn you. For I the Lord your God, the Holy One of Israel, and your Savior.

Isaiah 43:2-3 Holman CSB

My Priorities for Life

When I am worried, I try to think of things that I can do to help solve the things that trouble me.

I believe that it is important to try to live in "day-tight" compartments by not fretting too much about yesterday or tomorrow.

I find that the more I am able to trust God, the less worry I experience.

Check Your Priority		
High	Med.	Low
—	—	—
—	—	—
—	—	—

Stewardship of Your Time

Don't overlook the obvious here, friends. With God, one day is as good as a thousand years, a thousand years as a day.

2 Peter 3:8 MSG

Time is a nonrenewable gift from God. But sometimes, we treat our time here on earth as if it were not a gift at all: We may be tempted to invest our lives in trivial pursuits and mindless diversions. But our Father in heaven wants us to do more . . . much more.

Are you one of those people who puts things off until the last minute? Do you waste time doing things that don't matter very much while putting off the important things until it's too late to do the job right? If so, it's now time to start making better choices.

As you establish priorities for your day and your life, remember that each new day is a special treasure to be savored and celebrated. As a Christian, you have much to celebrate and much to do. It's up to you, and you alone, to honor God for the gift of time by using that gift wisely. Every day, like every life, is composed of moments. Each moment of your life holds within it the potential to seek God's will and to serve His purposes. If you are wise, you will strive to do both.

It may seem like you've got all the time in the world to do the things you need to do, but time is shorter than you think. Time here on earth is limited . . . use it or lose it!

Our time is short! The time we can invest for God, in creative things, in receiving our fellowmen for Christ, is short!

Billy Graham

Lord, tell me when the end will come and how long I will live. Let me know how long I have. You have given me only a short life; my lifetime is like nothing to you. Everyone's life is only a breath.

Psalm 39:4-5 NCV

PRIORITIES FOR MY LIFE

Finding time for God takes time . . . and it's up to you to find it. The world is constantly vying for your attention, and sometimes the noise can be deafening. Remember the words of Elisabeth Elliot; she said, "The world is full of noise. Let us learn the art of silence, stillness, and solitude."

TIMELESS WISDOM FOR GODLY LIVING

As we surrender the use of our time to the lordship of Christ, He will lead us to use it in the most productive way imaginable.

Charles Stanley

Over-commitment and time pressures are the greatest destroyers of marriages and families. It takes time to develop any friendship, whether with a loved one or with God himself.

James Dobson

Life's unfolding stops for no one.

Kathy Troccoli

The more time you give to something, the more you reveal its importance and value to you.

Rick Warren

> *There is an occasion for everything,*
> *and a time for every activity under heaven.*
> Ecclesiastes 3:1 Holman CSB

God has a present will for your life. It is neither chaotic nor utterly exhausting. In the midst of many good choices vying for your time, He will give you the discernment to recognize what is best.

Beth Moore

MORE WORDS FROM GOD'S WORD

So teach us to number our days, that we may gain a heart of wisdom.

Psalm 90:12 NKJV

Hard work means prosperity; only fools idle away their time.

Proverbs 12:11 NLT

We can't afford to waste a minute, must not squander these precious daylight hours in frivolity and indulgence, in sleeping around and dissipation, in bickering and grabbing everything in sight. Get out of bed and get dressed! Don't loiter and linger, waiting until the very last minute. Dress yourselves in Christ, and be up and about!

Romans 13:13-14 MSG

And the world with its lust is passing away, but the one who does God's will remains forever.

1 John 2:17 Holman CSB

My Priorities for Life

I believe that time is a nonrenewable resource that can be invested or squandered.

I understand the importance of setting priorities.

I understand that one form of stewardship is the stewardship of my time.

Check Your Priority		
High	Med.	Low
—	—	—
—	—	—
—	—	—

A Compelling Testimony: Yours

But the following night the Lord stood by him and said,
"Be of good cheer, Paul; for as you have testified for Me . . . ."

Acts 23:11 NKJV

Let's face facts: those of us who are Christians should be willing to talk about the things that Christ has done for us. Our personal testimonies are vitally important, but sometimes, because of shyness or insecurities, we're afraid to share our experiences. And that's unfortunate.

In his second letter to Timothy, Paul shares a message to believers of every generation when he writes, "God has not given us a spirit of timidity" (1:7). Paul's meaning is crystal clear: When sharing our testimonies, we must be courageous and unashamed.

We live in a world that desperately needs the healing message of Christ Jesus. Every believer, each in his or her own way, bears responsibility for sharing the Good News of our Savior. And it is important to remember that we bear testimony through both words and actions.

If you seek to be a faithful follower of Christ, then it's time for you to share your testimony with others. So today, preach the Gospel through your words and your deeds . . . but not necessarily in that order.

How many people have you made homesick for God?

Oswald Chambers

Theology is an interesting school of thought.
The Bible is beautiful literature. Sitting in a quiet sanctuary,
bathed in the amber light from stained-glass windows,
having our jangled nerves soothed by the chords from an organ—
all that is inspiring. But to tell you the truth, when we leave
the classroom, close the church door, and walk out into
the real world, it is the indisputable proof of
changed lives that makes us believers.

Gloria Gaither

PRIORITIES FOR MY LIFE

If your eternity with God is secure (because you believe in Jesus),
you have a profound responsibility to tell as many people as you
can about the eternal life that Christ offers to those who believe
in Him.

TIMELESS WISDOM FOR GODLY LIVING

Claim the joy that is yours. Pray. And know that your joy is used by God to reach others.

Kay Arthur

Faith in small things has repercussions that ripple all the way out. In a huge, dark room a little match can light up the place.

Joni Eareckson Tada

There is nothing more appealing or convincing to a watching world than to hear the testimony of someone who has just been with Jesus.

Henry Blackaby

But respect Christ as the holy Lord in your hearts.
Always be ready to answer everyone
who asks you to explain about the hope you have.
1 Peter 3:15 NCV

Those who are not yet in the family of Christ need us to be his hands, his feet, his eyes, his ears, and his voice to help them find God's love.

Doris Greig

MORE WORDS FROM GOD'S WORD

This and this only has been my appointed work: getting this news to those who have never heard of God, and explaining how it works by simple faith and plain truth.

1 Timothy 2:7 MSG

Therefore, we are ambassadors for Christ; certain that God is appealing through us, we plead on Christ's behalf, "Be reconciled to God."

2 Corinthians 5:20 Holman CSB

Proclaim the message; persist in it whether convenient or not; rebuke, correct, and encourage with great patience and teaching.

2 Timothy 4:2 Holman CSB

My Priorities for Life

	Check Your Priority		
	High	Med.	Low
I feel that my actions are as much a part of my testimony as my words.	—	—	—
I feel that my testimony has the power to change the world.	—	—	—
I believe that it is important to share my testimony.	—	—	—

Making All Things New

*The One who was sitting on the throne said,
"Look! I am making everything new!" Then he said,
"Write this, because these words are true and can be trusted."*

Revelation 21:5 NCV

Even the most inspired Christian teenagers can find themselves running on empty. Even people with the best intentions can run out of energy; even the most hopeful believers can be burdened by fears and doubts. And you're no exception.

When you're exhausted or worried, there is a source from which you can draw the power needed to recharge your spiritual batteries. That source is God.

God intends that His children lead joyous lives filled with abundance and peace. But sometimes, abundance and peace seem very far away. During these difficult days, we must turn to God for renewal, and when we do, He will restore us.

Are you tired or troubled? Turn your heart toward God in prayer. Are you weak or worried? Take the time—or, more accurately, make the time—to delve deeply into God's Holy Word. Are you spiritually depleted? Call upon fellow believers to support you, and call upon Christ to renew your spirit and

your life. When you do, you'll discover that the Creator of the
universe stands always ready and always able to create a new sense
of wonderment and joy in you.

He is the God of wholeness and restoration.

Stormie Omartian

PRIORITIES FOR MY LIFE

God wants to give you peace, and He wants to renew your spirit.
It's up to you to slow down and give Him a chance to do it.

TIMELESS WISDOM FOR GODLY LIVING

Christ came when all things were growing old. He made them new.

St. Augustine

But while relaxation is one thing, refreshment is another. We need to drink frequently and at length from God's fresh springs, to spend time in the Scripture, time in fellowship with Him, time worshiping Him.

Ruth Bell Graham

When we reach the end of our strength, wisdom, and personal resources, we enter into the beginning of his glorious provisions.

Patsy Clairmont

When doubts filled my mind, your comfort gave me renewed hope and cheer.
Psalm 94:19 NLT

In those desperate times when we feel like we don't have an ounce of strength, He will gently pick up our heads so that our eyes can behold something—something that will keep His hope alive in us.

Kathy Troccoli

MORE WORDS FROM GOD'S WORD

Create in me a pure heart, O God, and renew a steadfast spirit within me. Do not cast me from your presence or take your Holy Spirit from me. Restore to me the joy of your salvation and grant me a willing spirit, to sustain me.

Psalm 51:10-12 NIV

He makes me to lie down in green pastures; He leads me beside the still waters. He restores my soul; He leads me in the paths of righteousness For His name's sake.

Psalm 23:2–3 NKJV

You are being renewed in the spirit of your minds; you put on the new man, the one created according to God's likeness in righteousness and purity of the truth.

Ephesians 4:23-24 Holman CSB

My Priorities for Life

I understand the importance of getting a good night's sleep.

I believe that God can make all things new . . . including me.

I take time each day to be still and let God give me perspective and direction.

Check Your Priority		
High	Med.	Low
—	—	—
—	—	—
—	—	—

The Power of the Words We Speak

So then, rid yourselves of all evil, all lying, hypocrisy, jealousy,
and evil speech. As newborn babies want milk, you should want
the pure and simple teaching. By it you can grow up and be saved.

1 Peter 2:1-2 NCV

How important are the words we speak? More important than we may realize. Our words have echoes that extend beyond place or time. If our words are encouraging, we can lift others up; if our words are hurtful, we can hold others back.

Jesus said, "In everything, do to others what you would have them do to you, for this sums up the Law and the Prophets" (Matthew 7:12 NIV). This commandment is, indeed, the Golden Rule for Christians of every generation. And if we are to observe the Golden Rule, we must be careful to speak words of encouragement, hope, and truth to all those who cross our paths.

Do you want to be a source of encouragement to others? And, do you want to be a worthy ambassador for Christ? If so, you must speak words that are worthy of your Savior. So avoid angry outbursts. Refrain from impulsive outpourings. Terminate tantrums. Instead, speak words of encouragement and hope to your family and friends, who, by the way, need all the hope and encouragement they can find.

The battle of the tongue is won
not in the mouth,
but in the heart.

Annie Chapman

PRIORITIES FOR MY LIFE

When in doubt, use the Golden Rule to help you decide what to say: If you wouldn't like for somebody to say it about you, don't say it about them!

TIMELESS WISDOM FOR GODLY LIVING

Like dynamite, God's power is only latent power until it is released. You can release God's dynamite power into people's lives and the world through faith, your words, and prayer.

Bill Bright

Every word we speak, every action we take, has an effect on the totality of humanity. No one can escape that privilege—or that responsibility.

Laurie Beth Jones

The great test of a man's character is his tongue.

Oswald Chambers

Be gracious in your speech. The goal is to bring out the best in others in a conversation, not put them down, not cut them out.

Colossians 4:6 MSG

Perhaps we have been guilty of speaking against someone and have not realized how it may have hurt them. Then when someone speaks against us, we suddenly realize how deeply such words hurt, and we become sensitive to what we have done.

Theodore Epp

MORE WORDS FROM GOD'S WORD

To everything there is a season . . . a time to keep silence, and a time to speak.

Ecclesiastes 3:1,7 KJV

Watch the way you talk. Let nothing foul or dirty come out of your mouth. Say only what helps, each word a gift.

Ephesians 4:29 MSG

If anyone considers himself religious and yet does not keep a tight rein on his tongue, he deceives himself and his religion is worthless.

James 1:26 NIV

For the one who wants to love life and to see good days must keep his tongue from evil and his lips from speaking deceit.

1 Peter 3:10 Holman CSB

My Priorities for Life

Every day, I try to find at least one person to encourage.

I find that when I encourage others I, too, am encouraged.

I believe that my words are important, so I try to think before I speak, not after.

Check Your Priority		
High	Med.	Low
—	—	—
—	—	—
—	—	—

Optimistic Christianity

But if we look forward to something we don't have yet,
we must wait patiently and confidently.

Romans 8:25 NLT

Face facts: pessimism and Christianity don't mix. Why? Because Christians have every reason to be optimistic about life here on earth and life eternal. Mrs. Charles E. Cowman advised, "Never yield to gloomy anticipation. Place your hope and confidence in God. He has no record of failure."

Sometimes, despite our trust in God, we may fall into the spiritual traps of worry, frustration, anxiety, or sheer exhaustion, and our hearts become heavy. What's needed is plenty of rest, a large dose of perspective, and God's healing touch, but not necessarily in that order.

Today, make this promise to yourself and keep it: vow to be a hope-filled Christian. Think optimistically about your life, your education, your family, and your future. Trust your hopes, not your fears. Take time to celebrate God's glorious creation. And then, when you've filled your heart with hope, share your optimism with others. They'll be better for it, and so will you. But not necessarily in that order.

Keep your feet on the ground, but let your heart soar
as high as it will. Refuse to be average or to surrender
to the chill of your spiritual environment.

A. W. Tozer

The essence of optimism is that it takes no account of
the present, but it is a source of inspiration, of vitality,
and of hope. Where others have resigned, it enables a man to
hold his head high, to claim the future for himself,
and not abandon it to his enemy.

Dietrich Bonhoeffer

PRIORITIES FOR MY LIFE

Cynicism is contagious, and so is optimism. Choose your
thoughts and your friends accordingly.

TIMELESS WISDOM FOR GODLY LIVING

Hope looks for the good in people, opens doors for people, discovers what can be done to help, lights a candle, does not yield to cynicism. Hope sets people free.

Barbara Johnson

The people whom I have seen succeed best in life have always been cheerful and hopeful people who went about their business with a smile on their faces.

Charles Kingsley

Make the least of all that goes and the most of all that comes. Don't regret what is past. Cherish what you have. Look forward to all that is to come. And most important of all, rely moment by moment on Jesus Christ.

Gigi Graham Tchividjian

> *Make me hear joy and gladness.*
> Psalm 51:8 NKJV

Those who keep speaking about the sun while walking under a cloudy sky are messengers of hope, the true saints of our day.

Henri Nouwen

MORE WORDS FROM GOD'S WORD

My cup runs over. Surely goodness and mercy shall follow me all the days of my life; and I will dwell in the house of the Lord forever.

Psalm 23:5-6 NKJV

I can do everything through him that gives me strength.

Philippians 4:13 NIV

For God has not given us a spirit of fear, but of power and of love and of a sound mind.

2 Timothy 1:7 NLT

My Priorities for Life

	Check Your Priority	
High	Med.	Low

I will look for opportunities, not obstructions; and I will look for possibilities, not problems.

— — —

I will share words of encouragement and hope with my family, with my friends, and with others.

— — —

I understand the importance of counting my blessings, not my hardships.

— — —

I understand the need to associate with people who encourage me to be optimistic, upbeat, and cheerful.

— — —

Strength from Family

Choose for yourselves today the one you will worship . . . .
As for me and my family, we will worship the Lord.

Joshua 24:15 Holman CSB

Do you sometimes take your family for granted? If so, welcome to the club. At times, it's surprisingly easy to ignore the people we love the most. After all, we know that they'll still love us no matter what we do. But whenever we ignore our loved ones, we're doing a big disservice to them and to ourselves.

A loving family is a treasure from God. If God has blessed you with a close knit, supportive clan, offer a word of thanks to your Creator because He has given you one of His most precious earthly possessions. Your obligation, in response to God's gift, is to treat your family in ways that are consistent with His commandments.

You live in a fast-paced, demanding world, a place where life can be difficult and pressures can be intense. As those pressures build, you may tend to focus so intently upon your obligations that you lose sight, albeit temporarily, of your spiritual and emotional needs (that's one reason why a regular daily devotional time is so important; it offers a badly-needed dose of perspective).

So the next time your family life becomes a little stressful, remember this: That little band of men, women, kids, and babies is a priceless treasure on temporary loan from the Father above. And it's your responsibility to praise God for that gift—and to act accordingly.

When God asks someone to do something for Him entailing
sacrifice, He makes up for it in surprising ways.
Though He has led Bill all over the world to preach
the gospel, He has not forgotten the little family
in the mountains of North Carolina.

Ruth Bell Graham

PRIORITIES FOR MY LIFE

Since you love them, tell them so! Let your family members know that you love them by the things you say and the things you do. And, never take your family for granted; they deserve your very best treatment!

TIMELESS WISDOM FOR GODLY LIVING

Creating a warm, caring, supportive, encouraging environment is probably the most important thing you can do for your family.

Stephen Covey

Living life with a consistent spiritual walk deeply influences those we love most.

Vonette Bright

When you think about it for a moment, it certainly makes sense that if people can establish a loving and compatible relationship at home, they have a better chance of establishing winning relationships with those with whom they work on a regular basis.

Zig Ziglar

> *If a kingdom is divided against itself,*
> *that kingdom cannot stand. If a house is divided*
> *against itself, that house cannot stand.*
> Mark 3:24-25 Holman CSB

To maintain a joyful family requires much from both the parents and the children. Each member of the family has to become, in a special way, the servant of the others.

Pope John Paul II

MORE WORDS FROM GOD'S WORD

The one who brings ruin on his household will inherit the wind.

Proverbs 11:29 Holman CSB

Unless the Lord builds a house, its builders labor over it in vain; unless the Lord watches over a city, the watchman stays alert in vain.

Psalm 127:1 Holman CSB

Love must be without hypocrisy. Detest evil; cling to what is good. Show family affection to one another with brotherly love. Outdo one another in showing honor.

Romans 12:9–10 Holman CSB

Every kingdom divided against itself will be ruined, and every city or household divided against itself will not stand.

Matthew 12:25 NIV

My Priorities for Life

I think that my family should make God its number one priority.

I look for ways to say—and to show—my family I love them.

I place a high priority on spending time with my family.

Check Your Priority

High   Med.   Low

Too Many Questions?

If you don't know what you're doing, pray to the Father. He loves to help. You'll get his help, and won't be condescended to when you ask for it. Ask boldly, believingly, without a second thought. People who "worry their prayers" are like wind-whipped waves. Don't think you're going to get anything from the Master that way, adrift at sea, keeping all your options open.

James 1:5-8 MSG

Have you ever read the story about Moses trying to lead his people by following the will of God? If so, then you can plainly see that even a good man like Moses couldn't always understand the mysteries of God's plans. And neither can we. Sometimes, people who do nothing wrong get sick; sometimes, innocent people are hurt; sometimes, bad things happen to very good people. And just like Moses, we can't always understand why.

God doesn't explain Himself to us with the clarity that we humans would prefer (think about this: if God did explain Himself with perfect clarity, we wouldn't have enough brainpower to understand the explanation that He gave!).

When innocent people are hurt, we question God because we can't figure out exactly what He's doing, or why. Why are innocent people allowed to feel pain and good people allowed to die? Since we can't fully answer those kinds of questions now, we must trust in God's love, God's wisdom, and God's plan.

And while we're waiting for that wonderful day (in heaven) when all our questions will be answered, we should use the time that we have here on earth to help the people who need it most. After all, we'll have plenty of time to have our questions answered when we get to heaven. But when it comes to helping our neighbors, we don't have nearly that much time. So let's get busy helping . . . right now!

The Christian call . . . does not mean we are to become rigid and aggressive moralists with a strict and firm answer to every ethical problem. But it does mean we are committed to the conviction that there is an answer to be found.

David H. C. Read

PRIORITIES FOR MY LIFE

Too many questions? If you're faced with too many questions and too few answers, talk to God about it. When you do, you'll discover that He has more answers than you have questions.

TIMELESS WISDOM FOR GODLY LIVING

We are finding we don't have such a gnawing need to know the answers when we know the Answer.

Gloria Gaither

Questions allow us to grow and develop and change in our understanding of ourselves and of God, so that nothing that happens, and nothing that science discovers, is frightening, or disturbs our faith in God.

Madeleine L'Engle

An open mind, in questions that are not ultimate, is useful. But an open mind about the ultimate foundations either of Theoretical or of Practical Reason is idiocy.

C. S. Lewis

*Immediately the father of the boy cried out,
"I do believe! Help my unbelief."*
Mark 9:24 Holman CSB

Be to the world a sign that while we as Christians do not have all the answers, we do know and care about the questions.

Billy Graham

MORE WORDS FROM GOD'S WORD

When doubts filled my mind, your comfort gave me renewed hope and cheer.

Psalm 94:19 NLT

Jesus said, "Because you have seen Me, you have believed. Blessed are those who believe without seeing."

John 20:29 Holman CSB

Purify your hearts, ye double-minded.

James 4:8 KJV

Stop quarreling with God! If you agree with him, you will have peace at last, and things will go well for you.

Job 22:21 NLT

My Priorities for Life

As a way of dealing with my questions and worries, I find that I am helped by Bible study, prayer, and worship.

Check Your Priority
High   Med.   Low
—   —   —

When I have questions, I believe that it is important to take those questions to the Lord.

—   —   —

Even when I cannot understand why certain things happen, I trust God's plan for my life and the world.

—   —   —

The Power of Simplicity

"You've gotten a reputation as a bad-news people, you people of Judah and Israel, but I'm coming to save you. From now on, you're the good-news people. Don't be afraid. Keep a firm grip on what I'm doing."
Keep Your Lives Simple and Honest.

Zechariah 8:13 MSG

Y ou live in a world where simplicity is in short supply. Certainly, you are the beneficiary of many technological innovations, but these innovations have a price: in all likelihood, your world is highly complex. From the moment you wake up in the morning until the time you lay your head on the pillow at night, you are the target of an endless stream of audio and video. Many of these messages are intended to grab your attention in order to convince you to purchase things you didn't know you needed (and probably don't!). To make matters worse, many aspects of your life, including big stuff like education and health care, are caught in the undertow of an ever-increasing flood of government rules and regulations. So unless you take firm control of your time and your life, you may be overwhelmed by a tidal wave of red tape accompanied by a flood of distractions.

Is yours a life of moderation or accumulation? Are you more interested in the possessions you can acquire or in the person you can become? The answers to these questions will determine the direction of your day and, in time, the direction of your life.

If your material possessions are somehow distancing you from God, get rid of them. If your outside interests leave you too little time for your family or your faith, slow down the merry-go-round, or better yet, get off the merry-go-round completely. Remember: God wants your full attention, and He wants it today, so don't let anybody or anything get in His way.

In waiting we begin to get in touch with the rhythms of life—
stillness and action, listening and decision.
They are the rhythms of God. It is in the everyday
and the commonplace that we learn patience,
acceptance, and contentment.

Richard J. Foster

PRIORITIES FOR MY LIFE

Give simplicity a try now: Perhaps you think that the more stuff you acquire, the happier you'll be. If so, think again. Too much stuff means too many headaches, so start simplifying now.

TIMELESS WISDOM FOR GODLY LIVING

The most powerful life is the most simple life. The most powerful life is the life that knows where it's going, that knows where the source of strength is; it is the life that stays free of clutter and happenstance and hurriedness.

Max Lucado

In the name of Jesus Christ who was never in a hurry, we pray, O God, that You will slow us down, for we know that we live too fast. With all eternity before us, make us take time to live—time to get acquainted with You, time to enjoy Your blessing, and time to know each other.

Peter Marshall

Some of my greatest spiritual moments have been inspired by the unexpected and the simple.

Marilyn Meberg

A simple life in the Fear-of-God is better than a rich life with a ton of headaches.
Proverbs 15:16 MSG

Nobody is going to simplify your life for you. You've got to simplify things for yourself.

Marie T. Freeman

MORE WORDS FROM GOD'S WORD

But he's already made it plain how to live, what to do, what God is looking for in men and women. It's quite simple: Do what is fair and just to your neighbor, be compassionate and loyal in your love, and don't take yourself too seriously—take God seriously.

Micah 6:8 MSG

We brought nothing into the world, so we can take nothing out. But, if we have food and clothes, we will be satisfied with that.

1 Timothy 6:7-8 NCV

I deliberately kept it plain and simple: first Jesus and who he is; then Jesus and what he did—Jesus crucified.

1 Corinthians 2:2 MSG

My Priorities for Life

The world leads me toward a life of complexity and stress. God leads me toward simplicity and peace.

I understand that the accumulation of material possessions does not ensure a joyful life; it is my relationship with God (and my obedience to Him) that brings me abundance and joy.

I value the benefits of simplicity.

Check Your Priority		
High	Med.	Low
—	—	—
—	—	—
—	—	—

God's Gift of Grace

For the grace of God has been revealed, bringing salvation to all people. And we are instructed to turn from godless living and sinful pleasures. We should live in this evil world with self-control, right conduct, and devotion to God, while we look forward to that wonderful event when the glory of our great God and Savior, Jesus Christ, will be revealed.

Titus 2:11-12 NLT

God's grace is not earned . . . thank goodness! To earn God's love and His gift of eternal life would be far beyond the abilities of even the most righteous guys, girls, men, or women. Thankfully, grace is not an earthly reward for righteous behavior; it is an amazing spiritual gift which can be accepted by believers who dedicate themselves to God through Christ. When we accept Christ into our hearts, we are saved by His grace. And you don't need to be a Bible scholar to figure out that God's promise is right there in black and white on the pages of His Book (take a peak at Ephesians 2:8).

God's grace is the ultimate gift, and we owe to Him the ultimate in thanksgiving. So we should praise the Creator for His priceless gift, and we should share the Good News with all who cross our paths. We return our Father's love by accepting His grace and by sharing His message and His love.

Have you thanked God today for blessings that are too numerous to count? Have you offered Him your heartfelt prayers and your wholehearted praise? If not, it's time to slow down and offer a prayer of thanksgiving to the One who has given you life on earth and life eternal. No matter your circumstances, you owe God so much more than you can ever repay, and you owe Him your heartfelt thanks. So thank Him . . . and keep thanking Him, today, tomorrow and forever.

> ## Sin made us poor,
> ## but grace makes us rich.
>
> *Warren Wiersbe*

PRIORITIES FOR MY LIFE

God's grace is always available: Jim Cymbala writes, "No one is beyond His grace. No situation, anywhere on earth, is too hard for God." If you sincerely seek God's grace, He will give it freely. So ask, and you will receive.

TIMELESS WISDOM FOR GODLY LIVING

They travel lightly whom God's grace carries.

Thomas à Kempis

It's clear to me that our gossamer-thin lives are held together by the glue of God's grace.

Sheila Walsh

Grace grows better in the winter.

Samuel Rutherford

When we focus on God, the scene changes. He's in control of our lives; nothing lies outside the realm of His redemptive grace. Even when we make mistakes, fail in relationships, or deliberately make bad choices, God can redeem us.

Penelope J. Stokes

For if, by the trespass of the one man, death reigned through that one man, how much more will those who receive God's abundant provision of grace and of the gift of righteousness reign in life through the one man, Jesus Christ.
Romans 5:17 NIV

You will never be called upon to give anyone more grace than God has already given you.

Max Lucado

MORE WORDS FROM GOD'S WORD

For all have sinned and fall short of the glory of God, and are justified freely by his grace through the redemption that came by Christ Jesus.

Romans 3:23-24 NIV

But He gives more grace. Therefore He says: "God resists the proud, But gives grace to the humble."

James 4:6 NKJV

For it is by grace you have been saved, through faith—and this not from yourselves, it is the gift of God—not by works, so that no one can boast.

Ephesians 2:8-9 NIV

Let us then approach the throne of grace with confidence, so that we may receive mercy and find grace to help us in our time of need.

Hebrews 4:16 NIV

My Priorities for Life

	Check Your Priority	
High	Med.	Low

I believe that His grace is sufficient for my needs.

— — —

I believe in the importance of sharing the transforming message of God's gift of grace.

— — —

I believe that God has graced me with many gifts.

— — —

Becoming a Great Communicator

A wise man's heart guides his mouth, and his lips promote instruction.

Proverbs 16:23 NIV

Your skills as a communicator will have a profound impact upon your relationships, your career, and your life. The more quickly you learn how to communicate effectively, the more quickly you'll give yourself an instant jumpstart.

Would you like to become a better communicator? Here are a few simple rules that can help:

1. Think First, Speak Second: If you blurt out the first thing that comes into your head, you may say things that are better left unsaid. 2. Learn to be a Good Listener: If you want to be listened to, then you, too, must be a careful listener. 3. Don't be a Complainer: You simply can't whine your way to the top, so don't even try. 4. Don't Say Things "Behind Someone's Back" That You Wouldn't Say Directly to that Person's Face: Gossip isn't nice, and it isn't smart since the people you talk about will eventually find out what you said, and they won't forget. 5. Be a Trustworthy Communicator: Don't hedge the truth, don't omit important facts, and don't make promises that you can't keep. If you shade the truth, people always find out anyway, and they remember.

Today, make this promise to yourself: vow to be an honest, effective, encouraging communicator at school, at home, and everyplace in between. Speak wisely, not impulsively. Use words of kindness and praise, not words of anger or derision. Learn how to be truthful without being cruel. Remember that you have the power to heal others or to injure them, to lift others up or to hold them back. And when you learn how to lift them up, you'll soon discover that you've lifted yourself up, too.

We should ask ourselves three things
before we speak:
Is it true? Is it kind? Does it glorify God?

Billy Graham

PRIORITIES FOR MY LIFE

Want to be a better communicator? Try being a briefer communicator. Longwinded monologues, although satisfying to the speaker, are usually torture for the listener. So when in doubt, say less and listen more.

TIMELESS WISDOM FOR GODLY LIVING

Attitude and the spirit in which we communicate are as important as the words we say.

Charles Stanley

Part of good communication is listening with the eyes as well as with the ears.

Josh McDowell

The fewer words, the better prayer.

Martin Luther

Expressed affection is the best of all methods to use when you want to light a glow in someone's heart and to feel it in your own.

Ruth Stafford Peale

> *He who guards his mouth and his tongue*
> *keeps himself from calamity.*
> Proverbs 21:23 NIV

Does your message end with one point like a sword, or does it end like a broom with a thousand straws?

Vance Havner

MORE WORDS FROM GOD'S WORD

Do you see people who speak too quickly? There is more hope for a foolish person than for them.

Proverbs 29:20 NCV

A word fitly spoken is like apples of gold in settings of silver.

Proverbs 25:11 NKJV

May the words of my mouth and the meditation of my heart be pleasing in your sight, O LORD, my Rock and my Redeemer.

Psalm 19:14 NIV

Our Father is kind; you be kind. "Don't pick on people, jump on their failures, criticize their faults—unless, of course, you want the same treatment. Don't condemn those who are down; that hardness can boomerang. Be easy on people; you'll find life a lot easier.

Luke 6:36-37 MSG

My Priorities for Life

| | Check Your Priority | |
High	Med.	Low

I understand the need for honesty and candor.

—	—	—

I understand the need to be a good listener.

—	—	—

I understand the importance of being a good communicator.

—	—	—

During Those Difficult Days

We take the good days from God—
why not also the bad days?

Job 2:10 MSG

All of us face those occasional days when the traffic jams and the dog gobbles the homework. But, when we find ourselves overtaken by the minor frustrations of life, we must catch ourselves, take a deep breath, and lift our thoughts upward. Although we are here on earth struggling to rise above the distractions of the day, we need never struggle alone. God is here—eternally and faithfully, with infinite patience and love—and, if we reach out to Him, He will restore perspective and peace to our souls.

Sometimes even the most devout Christians can become discouraged, and you are no exception. After all, you live in a world where expectations can be high and demands can be even higher.

If you find yourself enduring difficult circumstances, remember that God remains in His heaven. If you become discouraged with the direction of your day or your life, lift your thoughts and prayers to Him. He is a God of possibility, not negativity. He will guide you through your difficulties and beyond them. Then, you can thank the Giver of all things good for blessings that are simply too numerous to count.

When life is difficult, God wants us
to have a faith that trusts and waits.

Kay Arthur

Faith does not eliminate problems.
Faith keeps you in a trusting relationship
with God in the midst of your problems.

Henry Blackaby

PRIORITIES FOR MY LIFE

If it weren't for trouble . . . we might think we could handle our lives by ourselves. Jim Cymbala writes, "Trouble is one of God's great servants because it reminds us how much we continually need the Lord." We should thank the Lord for challenges that bring us closer to Him.

TIMELESS WISDOM FOR GODLY LIVING

Anyone can carry his burden, however hard, until nightfall. Anyone can do his work, however hard, for one day. Anyone can live sweetly, patiently, lovingly, purely, till the sun goes down. And this is all that life really means.

Robert Louis Stevenson

Often, in the midst of great problems, we stop short of the real blessing God has for us, which is a fresh vision of who He is.

Anne Graham Lotz

The happiest people in the world are not those who have no problems, but the people who have learned to live with those things that are less than perfect.

James Dobson

We are hard pressed on every side, yet not crushed; we are perplexed, but not in despair.
2 Corinthians 4:8 NKJV

I choose joy. I will refuse the temptation to be cynical; cynicism is the tool of a lazy thinker. I will refuse to see people as anything less than human beings, created by God. I will refuse to see any problem as anything less than an opportunity to see God.

Max Lucado

MORE WORDS FROM GOD'S WORD

Now I take limitations in stride, and with good cheer, these limitations that cut me down to size—abuse, accidents, opposition, bad breaks. I just let Christ take over! And so the weaker I get, the stronger I become.

2 Corinthians 12:10 MSG

Consider it pure joy, my brothers, whenever you face trials of many kinds, because you know that the testing of your faith develops perseverance.

James 1:2-3 NIV

Whatever has been born of God conquers the world. This is the victory that has conquered the world: our faith.

1 John 5:4 Holman CSB

I took my troubles to the Lord; I cried out to him and he answered my prayer.

Psalm 120:1 NLT

My Priorities for Life

When I encounter difficulties, I work to solve the problems instead of worrying about them.

I tackle problems sooner rather than later.

When I encounter difficulties, I understand the importance of looking for solutions.

Check Your Priority		
High	Med.	Low
—	—	—
—	—	—
—	—	—

Claiming Contentment in a Discontented World

But godliness with contentment is great gain.
For we brought nothing into the world,
and we can take nothing out of it.
But if we have food and clothing, we will be content with that.

1 Timothy 6:6-8 NIV

Where can you find contentment? Is it a result of wealth or power or beauty or fame? Hardly. Genuine contentment springs from a peaceful spirit, a clear conscience, and a loving heart (like yours!).

Our modern world seems preoccupied with the search for happiness. We are bombarded with messages telling us that happiness depends upon the acquisition of material possessions. These messages are false. Enduring peace is not the result of our acquisitions; it is the inevitable result of our dispositions. If we don't find contentment within ourselves, we will never find it outside ourselves.

Thus the search for content is an internal quest, an exploration of the heart, mind, and soul. You can find contentment—indeed you will find it—if you simply look in the right places. And the best time to start looking in those places is now.

Are you a contented Christian? If so, then you are well aware of the healing power of the risen Christ. But if your spirit is temporarily troubled, perhaps you need to focus less upon your own priorities and more upon God's priorities. When you do, you'll rediscover this life-changing truth: Genuine contentment begins with God . . . and ends there.

When you accept rather than fight
your circumstances, even though you
don't understand them, you open your heart's gate
to God's love, peace, joy, and contentment.

Amy Carmichael

PRIORITIES FOR MY LIFE

Be contented where you are . . . even if it's not exactly where you want to end up. God has something wonderful in store for you—and remember that God's timing is perfect—so be patient, trust God, do your best, and expect the best.

TIMELESS WISDOM FOR GODLY LIVING

When we do what is right, we have contentment, peace, and happiness.

Beverly LaHaye

We are made for God, and nothing less will really satisfy us.

Brennan Manning

Father and Mother lived on the edge of poverty, and yet their contentment was not dependent upon their surroundings. Their relationship to each other and to the Lord gave them strength and happiness.

Corrie ten Boom

The secret of contentment in the midst of change is found in having roots in the changeless Christ—the same yesterday, today and forever.

Ed Young

Let your character be free from the love of money, being content with what you have; for He Himself has said, "I will never desert you, nor will I ever forsake you."
Hebrews 13:5 NASB

Contentment is possible when we stop striving for more.

Charles Swindoll

MORE WORDS FROM GOD'S WORD

A tranquil heart is life to the body, but jealousy is rottenness to the bones.

Proverbs 14:30 Holman CSB

Because your love is better than life, my lips will glorify you. I will praise you as long as I live, and in your name I will lift up my hands. My soul will be satisfied as with the richest of foods; with singing lips my mouth will praise you.

Psalm 63:3-5 NIV

How priceless is your unfailing love! Both high and low among men find refuge in the shadow of your wings. They feast on the abundance of your house; you give them drink from your river of delights. For with you is the fountain of life; in your light we see light.

Psalm 36:7-9 NIV

My Priorities for Life

| | Check Your Priority | |
High	Med.	Low

I understand that contentment comes, not from my circumstances, but from my attitude.

— — —

I understand that one way to find contentment is to praise God continually and thank Him for His blessings.

— — —

I believe that peace with God is the starting point for a contented life.

— — —

The Joys of Friendship

Greater love has no one than this,
that he lay down his life for his friends.

John 15:13 NIV

Some friendships help us honor God; these friendships should be nurtured. Other friendships place us in situations where we are tempted to dishonor God by disobeying His commandments; friendships such as these have the potential to do us great harm.

Because we tend to become like our friends, we must choose our friends carefully. Because our friends influence us in ways that are both subtle and powerful, we must ensure that our friendships are pleasing to God. When we spend our days in the presence of godly believers, we are blessed, not only by those friends, but also by our Creator.

Are you hanging out with people who make you a better Christian, or are you spending time with people who encourage you to stray from your faith? The answer to this question will have a surprising impact on the condition of your spiritual health. Why? Because peer pressure is very real and very powerful. So, one of the best ways to ensure that you follow

Christ is to find fellow believers who are willing to follow Him with you.

Many elements of society seek to mold you into a more worldly being; God, on the other hand, seeks to mold you into a new being, a new creation through Christ, a being that is most certainly not conformed to this world. If you are to please God, you must resist the pressures that society seeks to impose upon you, and you must choose, instead, to follow in the footsteps of His only begotten Son.

Some people come into our lives and quickly go. Some people stay for awhile and leave footprints on our hearts, and we are never the same.

Anonymous

PRIORITIES FOR MY LIFE

Remember the first rule of friendship: it's the Golden one, and it starts like this: "Do unto others . . ." (Matthew 7:12)

TIMELESS WISDOM FOR GODLY LIVING

Inasmuch as anyone pushes you nearer to God, he or she is your friend.

Barbara Johnson

God often keeps us on the path by guiding us through the counsel of friends and trusted spiritual advisors.

Bill Hybels

Friendship is one of the sweetest joys of life. Many might have failed beneath the bitterness of their trial had they not found a friend.

C. H. Spurgeon

A friend loves you all the time,
and a brother helps in time of trouble.
Proverbs 17:17 NCV

Though I know intellectually how vulnerable I am to pride and power, I am the last one to know when I succumb to their seduction. That's why spiritual Lone Rangers are so dangerous— and why we must depend on trusted brothers and sisters who love us enough to tell us the truth.

Chuck Colson

MORE WORDS FROM GOD'S WORD

As iron sharpens iron, a friend sharpens a friend.

Proverbs 27:17 NLT

If a fellow believer hurts you, go and tell him—work it out between the two of you. If he listens, you've made a friend.

Matthew 18:15 MSG

Beloved, if God so loved us, we also ought to love one another.

1 John 4:11 NKJV

I give thanks to my God for every remembrance of you.

Philippians 1:3 Holman CSB

My Priorities for Life

	Check Your Priority	
High	Med.	Low

Because I want to cultivate my friendships, I make the effort to spend time with my friends.

— — —

I understand the importance of building close friendships.

— — —

In building friendships, I emphasize the need for mutual honesty and mutual trust.

— — —

Acceptance for Today

A man's heart plans his way, but the Lord determines his steps.

Proverbs 16:9 Holman CSB

The American theologian Reinhold Niebuhr composed a profoundly simple verse that came to be known as the Serenity Prayer: "God, grant me the serenity to accept the things I cannot change, the courage to change the things I can, and the wisdom to know the difference." Niebuhr's words are far easier to recite than they are to live by. Why? Because most of us want life to unfold in accordance with our own wishes and timetables. But sometimes God has other plans.

Author Hannah Whitall Smith observed, "How changed our lives would be if we could only fly through the days on wings of surrender and trust!" These words remind us that even when we cannot understand the workings of God, we must trust Him and accept His will.

So if you've encountered unfortunate circumstances that are beyond your power to control, accept those circumstances . . . and trust God. When you do, you can be comforted in the knowledge that your Creator is both loving and wise, and that He understands His plans perfectly, even when you do not.

I am truly grateful that faith enables me
to move past the question of "Why?"

Zig Ziglar

*The Lord says, "Forget what happened before, and do not think
about the past. Look at the new thing I am going to do.
It is already happening. Don't you see it? I will make
a road in the desert and rivers in the dry land."*

Isaiah 43:18-19 NCV

PRIORITIES FOR MY LIFE

You should learn from the past, but you should never allow
yourself to become stuck there. Once you have made peace with
the past, you are free to live more fully in the present . . . and
that's precisely what you should do.

TIMELESS WISDOM FOR GODLY LIVING

Prayer may not get us what we want, but it will teach us to want what we need.

Vance Havner

What cannot be altered must be borne, not blamed.

Thomas Fuller

The key to contentment is to consider. Consider who you are and be satisfied with that. Consider what you have and be satisfied with that. Consider what God's doing and be satisfied with that.

Luci Swindoll

If we know we have pleased God, contentment will be our consolation, for what pleases God will please us.

Kay Arthur

For everything created by God is good, and nothing should be rejected if it is received with thanksgiving.

1 Timothy 4:4 Holman CSB

We need to be at peace with our past, content with our present, and sure about our future, knowing they are all in God's hands.

Joyce Meyer

MORE WORDS FROM GOD'S WORD

Should we accept only good from God and not adversity?

Job 2:10 Holman CSB

Come to terms with God and be at peace; in this way good will come to you.

Job 22:21 Holman CSB

Sheathe your sword! Should I not drink the cup that the Father has given Me?

John 18:11 Holman CSB

He is the Lord. Let him do what he thinks is best.

1 Samuel 3:18 NCV

My Priorities for Life

	Check Your Priority		
	High	Med.	Low
I think it is important to change what I need to change and accept that which I can't change.	—	—	—
I think it is important to learn from the past, to accept the past, and to live in the present.	—	—	—
I believe that it is important to trust God even when I don't understand why certain things happen.	—	—	—

The Value of Hard Work

In all the work you are doing, work the best you can.
Work as if you were doing it for the Lord, not for people.

Colossians 3:23 NCV

Have you acquired the habit of doing first things first, or are you one of those guys (or girls) who put off important work until the last minute? The answer to this simple question will help determine how well you do your work and how much fun you have doing it.

God's Word teaches us the value of hard work. In his second letter to the Thessalonians, Paul warns, " . . . if any would not work, neither should he eat" (3:10 KJV). And the Book of Proverbs proclaims, "One who is slack in his work is brother to one who destroys" (18:9 NIV). In short, God has created a world in which diligence is rewarded and laziness is not. So, whatever it is that you choose to do, do it with commitment, excitement, and vigor. And remember this: Hard work is not simply a proven way to get ahead; it's also part of God's plan for you.

You have countless opportunities to accomplish great things for God—but you should not expect the work to be easy. So pray as if everything depended upon God, but work as if everything depended upon you. When you do, you should expect very big payoffs because when you and God become partners in your work, amazing things happen.

God does not want us to work for Him, nor does He want to be our helper. Rather, He wants to do His work in and through us.

Vonette Bright

PRIORITIES FOR MY LIFE

Goofing off is contagious. That's why it's important for you to hang out with people who are interested in getting the job done right—and getting it done right now!

TIMELESS WISDOM FOR GODLY LIVING

Help yourself and God will help you.

St. Joan of Arc

Think enthusiastically about everything, especially your work.

Norman Vincent Peale

Hoping for a good future without investing in today is like a farmer waiting for a crop without ever planting any seed.

John Maxwell

I long to accomplish a great and noble task, but it is my chief duty to accomplish small tasks as if they were great and noble.

Helen Keller

Then He said to His disciples,
"The harvest truly is plentiful, but the laborers are few."
Matthew 9:37 NKJV

The higher the ideal, the more work is required to accomplish it. Do not expect to become a great success in life if you are not willing to work for it.

Father Flanagan

MORE WORDS FROM GOD'S WORD

The people had a mind to work.

Nehemiah 4:6 KJV

But as for you, be strong and do not give up, for your work will be rewarded.

2 Chronicles 15:7 NIV

Work hard so God can say to you, "Well done." Be a good workman, one who does not need to be ashamed when God examines your work . . . .

2 Timothy 2:15 TLB

But one thing I do: Forgetting what is behind and straining toward what is ahead, I press on toward the goal to win the prize for which God has called me heavenward in Christ Jesus.

Philippians 3:13-14 NIV

My Priorities for Life

I believe that I am working, not just for myself, but also for God.

I believe that the way that I accomplish my job serves as an important example to others.

I believe that my work is important and that it deserves my best effort.

Check Your Priority		
High	Med.	Low
—	—	—
—	—	—
—	—	—

On Beyond Failure

We are hard pressed on every side, yet not crushed;
we are perplexed, but not in despair.

2 Corinthians 4:8 NKJV

Mary Pickford was "America's sweetheart" in the early days of motion pictures. Miss Pickford had a simple yet powerful formula for success: She said, "This thing we call 'failure' is not falling down, but staying down." Miss Pickford might have added that every time we get back up, we build character.

Life's occasional setbacks are simply the price that we must pay for our willingness to take risks as we follow our dreams. But even when we encounter bitter disappointments, we must never lose faith.

Hebrews 10:36 advises, "Patient endurance is what you need now, so you will continue to do God's will. Then you will receive all that he has promised" (NLT). These words remind us that when we persevere, we will eventually receive the rewards which God has promised us. What's required is perseverance, not perfection.

When we face hardships and disappointments, God stands ready to protect us. Our responsibility, of course, is to ask Him for protection. When we call upon Him in heartfelt prayer, He will answer—in His own time and according to His own plan—and He will do His part to heal us. We, of course, must do our part, too.

And, while we are waiting for God's plans to unfold and for His healing touch to restore us, we can be comforted in the knowledge that our Creator can overcome any obstacle, even if we cannot.

> The difference between winning and losing
> is how we choose to react to disappointment.
>
> *Barbara Johnson*

PRIORITIES FOR MY LIFE

Failure isn't permanent . . . unless you fail to bounce back. So pick yourself up, dust yourself off, and trust God. He will make it right. Warren Wiersbe had this advice: "No matter how badly we have failed, we can always get up and begin again. Our God is the God of new beginnings." And don't forget: the best time to begin again is now.

TIMELESS WISDOM FOR GODLY LIVING

What may seem defeat to us may be victory to him.

C. H. Spurgeon

Recently I've been learning that life comes down to this: God is in everything. Regardless of what difficulties I am experiencing at the moment, or what things aren't as I would like them to be, I look at the circumstances and say, "Lord, what are you trying to teach me?"

Catherine Marshall

Every achievement worth remembering is stained with the blood of diligence and scarred by the wounds of disappointment.

Charles Swindoll

> *Sometimes I ask God, my rock-solid God,*
> *"Why did you let me down? Why am I walking*
> *around in tears, harassed by enemies?"*
> Psalm 42:9 MSG

Why should I ever resist any delay or disappointment, any affliction or oppression or humiliation, when I know God will use it in my life to make me like Jesus and to prepare me for heaven?

Kay Arthur

MORE WORDS FROM GOD'S WORD

Is anyone among you suffering? Then he must pray.

James 5:13 NASB

These things I have spoken to you, that in Me you may have peace. In the world you will have tribulation; but be of good cheer, I have overcome the world.

John 16:33 NKJV

Sometimes I ask God, my rock-solid God, "Why did you let me down? Why am I walking around in tears, harassed by enemies?"

Psalm 42:9 MSG

But as for you, be strong; don't be discouraged, for your work has a reward.

2 Chronicles 15:7 Holman CSB

My Priorities for Life

	Check Your Priority	
High	Med.	Low

I believe that I have much to learn from adversity.

— — —

I believe that adversity can be a stepping stone to success.

— — —

I value the need to keep my disappointments in perspective.

— — —

The Value of Your Daily Devotional

Morning by morning he wakens me and opens my understanding to his will. The Sovereign Lord has spoken to me, and I have listened.

Isaiah 50:4-5 NLT

When it comes to spending time with God, are you a "squeezer" or a "pleaser"? Do you squeeze God into your schedule with a prayer before meals (and maybe, if you've got the time, with a quick visit to church on Sunday)? Or do you please God by talking to Him far more often than that? The answer to this question will determine the direction of your day and the quality of your life.

Each day has 1,440 minutes—do you value your relationship with God enough to spend a few of those minutes with Him? He deserves that much of your time and more—is He receiving it from you? Hopefully so. But if you find that you're simply "too busy" for a daily chat with your Father in heaven, it's time to take a long, hard look at your priorities and your values.

Warren Wiersbe writes, "Surrender your mind to the Lord at the beginning of each day." And that's sound advice. When you begin each day with your head bowed and your heart lifted, you are reminded of God's love, His protection, and His commandments. Then, you can align your priorities for the coming day with the teachings and commandments that God has placed upon your heart.

So, if you've acquired the unfortunate habit of trying to squeeze God into the corners of your life, it's time to reshuffle the items on your to-do list by placing God first. God wants your undivided attention, not the leftovers of your day. And if you haven't already done so, form the habit of spending quality time with your Father in heaven. He deserves it . . . and so, for that matter, do you.

Every day has its own particular brand of holiness
to discover and worship appropriately.

Annie Dillard

PRIORITIES FOR MY LIFE

How much time can you spare? Decide how much of your time God deserves, and then give it to Him. Don't organize your day so that God gets "what's left." Give Him what you honestly believe He deserves.

TIMELESS WISDOM FOR GODLY LIVING

Meditating upon His Word will inevitably bring peace of mind, strength of purpose, and power for living.

Bill Bright

Make a plan now to keep a daily appointment with God. The enemy is going to tell you to set it aside, but you must carve out the time. If you're too busy to meet with the Lord, friend, then you are simply too busy.

Charles Swindoll

How motivating it has been for me to view my early morning devotions as a time of retreat alone with Jesus, Who desires that I "come with Him by myself to a quiet place" in order to pray, read His Word, listen for His voice, and be renewed in my spirit.

Anne Graham Lotz

It is good to give thanks to the Lord, to sing praises to the Most High. It is good to proclaim your unfailing love in the morning, your faithfulness in the evening.

Psalm 92:1-2 NLT

Every morning is a fresh opportunity to find God's extraordinary joy in the most ordinary places.

Janet. L. Weaver

MORE WORDS FROM GOD'S WORD

But grow in the grace and knowledge of our Lord and Savior Jesus Christ. To Him be the glory both now and to the day of eternity.

2 Peter 3:18 Holman CSB

Truly my soul silently waits for God; from Him comes my salvation.

Psalm 62:1 NKJV

May the words of my mouth and the thoughts of my heart be pleasing to you, O Lord, my rock and my redeemer.

Psalm 19:14 NLT

Be still, and know that I am God.

Psalm 46:10 NKJV

My Priorities for Life

I try to listen carefully to the things that God places upon my heart.

I have a regular time and place where I can read, pray, and talk to God.

I understand the importance of spending time each day with God.

Check Your Priority		
High	Med.	Low
—	—	—
—	—	—
—	—	—

The Power of Hope

The lines of purpose in your lives never grow slack,
tightly tied as they are to your future in heaven, kept taut by hope.

Colossians 1:5 MSG

There are few sadder sights on earth than the sight of a girl or a guy who has lost hope. In difficult times, hope can be elusive, but those who place their faith in God's promises need never lose it. After all, God is good; His love endures; He has promised His children the gift of eternal life. And, God keeps His promises.

Despite God's promises, despite Christ's love, and despite our countless blessings, we're only human, and we can still lose hope from time to time. When we do, we need the encouragement of Christian friends, the life-changing power of prayer, and the healing truth of God's Holy Word.

If you find yourself falling into the spiritual traps of worry and discouragement, seek the healing touch of Jesus and the encouraging words of fellow believers. And if you find a friend in need, remind him or her of the peace that is found through a genuine relationship with Christ. It was Christ who promised, "I have told you these things so that in Me you may have peace. In the world you have suffering. But take courage! I have conquered the world" (John 16:33 Holman CSB). This world can be a place of trials and troubles, but as believers, we are secure. God has promised us peace, joy, and eternal life. And, of course, God keeps His promises today, tomorrow, and forever.

> # Hope is a wonderful thing—
> # one little nibble
> # will keep a man fishing all day.
>
> *Barbara Johnson*

Are you a Christian? If you are, how can you be hopeless? Are you so depressed by the greatness of your problems that you have given up all hope? Instead of giving up, would you patiently endure? Would you focus on Christ until you are so preoccupied with him alone that you fall prostrate before him?

Anne Graham Lotz

PRIORITIES FOR MY LIFE

Never be afraid to hope—or to ask—for a miracle.

TIMELESS WISDOM FOR GODLY LIVING

Easter comes each year to remind us of a truth that is eternal and universal. The empty tomb of Easter morning says to you and me, "Of course you'll encounter trouble. But behold a God of power who can take any evil and turn it into a door of hope."

Catherine Marshall

When you say a situation or a person is hopeless, you are slamming the door in the face of God.

Charles Allen

Nothing in this world is more fundamental for success in life than hope, and this star pointed to our only source of true hope: Jesus Christ.

D. James Kennedy

Let us hold fast the confession of our hope without wavering, for He who promised is faithful.
Hebrews 10:23 NASB

Hope is the desire and the ability to move forward.

Emilie Barnes

MORE WORDS FROM GOD'S WORD

This hope we have as an anchor of the soul, a hope both sure and steadfast.

Hebrews 6:19 NASB

Full of hope, you'll relax, confident again; you'll look around, sit back, and take it easy.

Job 11:18 MSG

The Lord is good to those whose hope is in him, to the one who seeks him; it is good to wait quietly for the salvation of the Lord.

Lamentations 3:25-26 NIV

May the God of hope fill you with all joy and peace as you trust in him, so that you may overflow with hope by the power of the Holy Spirit.

Romans 15:13 NIV

My Priorities for Life

	Check Your Priority		
	High	Med.	Low
I believe that God offers me "a peace that passes understanding," and I desire to accept God's peace.	—	—	—
I understand that action is an antidote to worry.	—	—	—
I believe that genuine hope begins with hope in a sovereign God.	—	—	—

The Size of Your Problems

All I'm doing right now, friends, is showing how these things pertain to Apollos and me so that you will learn restraint and not rush into making judgments without knowing all the facts. It is important to look at things from God's point of view. I would rather not see you inflating or deflating reputations based on mere hearsay.

1 Corinthians 4:6 MSG

Here's a riddle: What is it that is too unimportant to pray about yet too big for God to handle? The answer, of course, is: "nothing." Yet sometimes, when the challenges of the day seem overwhelming, we may spend more time worrying about our troubles than praying about them. And, we may spend more time fretting about our problems than solving them. A far better strategy, of course, is to pray as if everything depended entirely upon God and to work as if everything depended entirely upon us.

Life is an exercise in problem-solving. The question is not whether we will encounter problems; the real question is how we will choose to address them. When it comes to solving the problems of everyday living, we often know precisely what needs to be done, but we may be slow in doing it—especially if what needs to be done is difficult or uncomfortable for us. So we put off till tomorrow what should be done today.

The words of Psalm 34 remind us that the Lord solves problems for "people who do what is right." And usually, "doing what is right" means doing the uncomfortable work of confronting our problems sooner rather than later. So with no further ado, let the problem-solving begin . . . now!

Earthly fears are no fears at all. Answer the big question of eternity, and the little questions of life fall into perspective.

Max Lucado

PRIORITIES FOR MY LIFE

Keep life in perspective: Your life is an integral part of God's grand plan. So don't become unduly upset over the minor inconveniences of life, and don't worry too much about today's setbacks—they're temporary.

TIMELESS WISDOM FOR GODLY LIVING

The Bible is a remarkable commentary on perspective. Through its divine message, we are brought face to face with issues and tests in daily living and how, by the power of the Holy Spirit, we are enabled to respond positively to them.

Luci Swindoll

Instead of being frustrated and overwhelmed by all that is going on in our world, go to the Lord and ask Him to give you His eternal perspective.

Kay Arthur

Joy is the direct result of having God's perspective on our daily lives and the effect of loving our Lord enough to obey His commands and trust His promises.

Bill Bright

Since you have been raised to new life with Christ, set your sights on the realities of heaven, where Christ sits at God's right hand in the place of honor and power.

Colossians 3:1 NLT

Mature people are not emotionally and spiritually devastated by every mistake they make. They are able to maintain some kind of balance in their lives.

Joyce Meyer

MORE WORDS FROM GOD'S WORD

First pay attention to me, and then relax. Now you can take it easy—you're in good hands.

Proverbs 1:33 MSG

The thing you should want most is God's kingdom and doing what God wants. Then all these other things you need will be given to you.

Matthew 6:33 NCV

It's obvious, isn't it? The place where your treasure is, is the place you will most want to be, and end up being.

Luke 12:34 MSG

Let us fix our eyes on Jesus, the author and perfecter of our faith, who for the joy set before him endured the cross, scorning its shame, and sat down at the right hand of the throne of God.

Hebrews 12:2 NIV

My Priorities for Life

	Check Your Priority	
High	Med.	Low

When I encounter problems, I will also look for solutions.

— — —

I will not overestimate the size of my problems.

— — —

When I encounter problems, I will tackle them sooner rather than later.

— — —

Trusting His Timetable

To everything there is a season, a time for every purpose under heaven.

Ecclesiastes 3:1 NKJV

Are you a guy or girl in a hurry? If so, you're probably not the only one in your neighborhood. We human beings are, by our very nature, impatient. We are impatient with others, impatient with ourselves, and impatient with our Creator. We want things to happen according to our own timetables, but our Heavenly Father may have other plans. That's why we must learn the art of patience.

All too often, we are unwilling to trust God's perfect timing. We allow ourselves to become apprehensive and anxious as we wait nervously for God to act. Usually, we know what we want, and we know precisely when we want it: right now, if not sooner. But, when God's plans differ from our own, we must train ourselves to trust in His infinite wisdom and in His infinite love.

As people living in a fast-paced world, many of us find that waiting quietly for God is quite troubling. But in our better moments, we realize that patience is not only a virtue; it is also a commandment from the Creator.

Psalm 37:7 makes it clear that we should "Be still before the Lord and wait patiently for Him" (NIV). But ours is a generation that usually places little value on stillness and patience. No matter. God instructs us to be patient in all things, and we must obey Him or suffer the consequences of His displeasure.

We must be patient with our families, with our friends, and with ourselves. We must also be patient with our Heavenly Father as He shapes our world (and our lives) in accordance with His timetable, not our own. And that's as it should be. After all, think how patient God has been with us.

God never hurries.
There are no deadlines against which He must work.
To know this is to quiet our spirits and relax our nerves.

A. W. Tozer

PRIORITIES FOR MY LIFE

Trust God's timing. God has very big plans in store for you, so trust Him and wait patiently for those plans to unfold. And remember: God's timing is best, so don't allow yourself to become discouraged if things don't work out exactly as you wish. Instead of worrying about your future, entrust it to God. He knows exactly what you need and exactly when you need it.

TIMELESS WISDOM FOR GODLY LIVING

God is in no hurry. Compared to the works of mankind, He is extremely deliberate. God is not a slave to the human clock.

Charles Swindoll

Waiting on God brings us to the journey's end quicker than our feet.

Mrs. Charles E. Cowman

When we read of the great Biblical leaders, we see that it was not uncommon for God to ask them to wait, not just a day or two, but for years, until God was ready for them to act.

Gloria Gaither

This is what the LORD says:
"In the time of my favor I will answer you,
and in the day of salvation I will help you . . . ."
Isaiah 49:8 NIV

He whose attitude towards Christ is correct does indeed ask "in His Name" and receives what he asks for if it is something which does not stand in the way of his salvation. He gets it, however, only when he ought to receive it, for certain things are not refused us, but their granting is delayed to a fitting time.

St. Augustine

MORE WORDS FROM GOD'S WORD

Humble yourselves, therefore, under God's mighty hand, that he may lift you up in due time.

1 Peter 5:6 NIV

From one man he made every nation of men, that they should inhabit the whole earth; and he determined the times set for them and the exact places where they should live.

Acts 17:26 NIV

Wait for the LORD; be strong and take heart and wait for the LORD.

Psalm 27:14 NIV

I wait for the LORD, my soul waits, and in his word I put my hope.

Psalm 130:5 NIV

My Priorities for Life

I believe that patience is not idle waiting but that it is an activity that means being watchful as I wait for God to lead me.

Even when I don't understand the circumstances that confront me, I strive to wait patiently while serving the Lord.

I take seriously the Bible's instructions to be patient.

Check Your Priority		
High	Med.	Low
—	—	—
—	—	—
—	—	—

Beyond Loneliness

I am not alone, because the Father is with Me.

John 16:32 NKJV

If you're like most people, you've experienced occasional bouts of loneliness. If so, you understand the genuine pain that accompanies those feelings that "nobody cares." In truth, lots of people care about you, but at times, you may hardly notice their presence.

Sometimes, intense feelings of loneliness may be the result of depression (if you think this might be the case, talk things over with your family, with your pastor, and with your physician). Other times, however, your feelings of loneliness come as a result of your own hesitation, the hesitation to "get out there and make new friends."

Why do so many of us hesitate to meet new people and make new friends? Several reasons: some of us are just plain shy, and because of our shyness, we find it more difficult to interact with unfamiliar people. Others, while not exceedingly shy, are overly attuned to the potential of rejection. Still others may be so self-critical that they feel unworthy of the attentions of others.

In truth, the world is literally teeming with people who are looking for new friends. And yet, ironically enough, too many of us allow our friendships to wither away, not because we intentionally alienate others, but because we simply don't pay enough attention to them.

The philosopher William James observed, "Human beings are born into this little span of life, and among the best things that life has to offer are its friendships and intimacies. Yet, humans leave their friendships with no cultivation, letting them grow as they will by the roadside." James understood that when we leave our friendships unattended, the resulting harvest is predictably slim. Don't let it happen to you!

> # Loneliness is the first thing which God's eye named not good.
>
> *John Milton*

PRIORITIES FOR MY LIFE

Want to meet more people? Become more involved in your church or in community service: they'll welcome your participation, and you'll welcome the chance to connect with more and more people.

TIMELESS WISDOM FOR GODLY LIVING

We are born helpless. As soon as we are fully conscious we discover loneliness. We need others physically, emotionally, intellectually; we need them if we are to know anything, even ourselves.

C. S. Lewis

When we are living apart for God, we can be lonely and lost, even in the midst of a crowd.

Billy Graham

Are you feeling lonely today because of suffering? My word to you is simply this: Jesus Christ is there with you.

Warren Wiersbe

The Lord is near all who call out to Him,
all who call out to Him with integrity.
He fulfills the desires of those who fear Him;
He hears their cry for help and saves them.
Psalm 145:18-19 Holman CSB

Sometimes the loveliness of God's presence comes in the midst of pain.

Madeleine L'Engle

MORE WORDS FROM GOD'S WORD

I have set the Lord always before me; because He is at my right hand I shall not be moved.

Psalm 16:8 NKJV

The Lord Almighty is here among us; the God of Israel is our fortress. Come see the glorious works of the Lord . . . .

Psalm 46:7-8 NLT

Come near to God, and God will come near to you. You sinners, clean sin out of your lives. You who are trying to follow God and the world at the same time, make your thinking pure.

James 4:8 NCV

My Priorities for Life

	Check Your Priority	
High	Med.	Low

When I feel lonely, I understand that the feeling is temporary.

— — —

I know that I am never alone because God is always near.

— — —

I understand that making friends—and keeping friends—often requires effort on my part.

— — —

The Right Kind of Attitude

Set your mind on things above, not on things on the earth.

Colossians 3:2 NKJV

Of course you've heard the saying, "Life is what you make it." And although that statement may seem very trite, it's also very true. You can choose a life filled to the brim with frustration and fear, or you can choose a life of abundance and peace. That choice is up to you—and only you— and it depends, to a surprising extent, upon your attitude.

What's your attitude today? Are you fearful, angry, bored, or worried? Are you pessimistic, perplexed, pained, and perturbed? Are you moping around with a frown on your face that's almost as big as the one in your heart? If so, God wants to have a little talk with you.

God created you in His own image, and He wants you to experience joy, contentment, peace, and abundance. But, God will not force you to experience these things; you must claim them for yourself.

God has given you free will, including the ability to influence the direction and the tone of your thoughts. And, here's how God wants you to direct those thoughts:

"Finally brothers, whatever is true, whatever is honorable, whatever is just, whatever is pure, whatever is lovely, whatever is commendable—if there is any moral excellence and if there is any praise—dwell on these things" (Philippians 4:8 Holman CSB).

The quality of your attitude will help determine the quality of your life, so you must guard your thoughts accordingly. If you make up your mind to approach life with a healthy mixture of realism and optimism, you'll be rewarded. But, if you allow yourself to fall into the unfortunate habit of negative thinking, you will doom yourself to unhappiness or mediocrity, or worse.

So, the next time you find yourself dwelling upon the negative aspects of your life, refocus your attention on things positive. The next time you find yourself falling prey to the blight of pessimism, stop yourself and turn your thoughts around. The next time you're tempted to waste valuable time gossiping or complaining, resist those temptations with all your might.

And remember: You'll never whine your way to the top . . . so don't waste your breath.

What is the difference between an obstacle and an opportunity? Our attitude toward it. Every opportunity has a difficulty, and every difficulty has an opportunity.

J. Sidlow Baxter

PRIORITIES FOR MY LIFE

Have a happy heart every day. And remember that you can choose to have a good attitude or a not-so good attitude. And it's a choice you make every day.

TIMELESS WISDOM FOR GODLY LIVING

The greater part of our happiness or misery depends on our dispositions, and not on our circumstances.

Martha Washington

Feelings of confidence depend upon the type of thoughts you habitually occupy. Think defeat, and you are bound to be defeated.

Norman Vincent Peale

The things we think are the things that feed our souls. If we think on pure and lovely things, we shall grow pure and lovely like them; and the converse is equally true.

Hannah Whitall Smith

Come near to God, and God will come near to you. You sinners, clean sin out of your lives. You who are trying to follow God and the world at the same time, make your thinking pure.

James 4:8 NCV

It's your choice: you can either count your blessings or recount your disappointments.

Jim Gallery

MORE WORDS FROM GOD'S WORD

Finally, brethren, whatever is true, whatever is honorable, whatever is right, whatever is pure, whatever is lovely, whatever is of good repute, if there is any excellence and if anything worthy of praise, dwell on these things.

Philippians 4:8 NASB

So prepare your minds for service and have self-control.

1 Peter 1:13 NCV

A miserable heart means a miserable life; a cheerful heart fills the day with a song.

Proverbs 15:15 MSG

My Priorities for Life

I believe that it is important to associate myself with people who are upbeat, optimistic, and encouraging.

I believe that it is important to focus my thoughts on the positive aspects of life, not the negative ones.

I believe that if I want to change certain aspects of my life, I also need to make adjustments in my own attitudes toward life.

Check Your Priority		
High	Med.	Low
—	—	—
—	—	—
—	—	—

Cheerful Christianity

*Jacob said, "For what a relief it is to see your friendly smile.
It is like seeing the smile of God!"*

Genesis 33:10 NLT

Cheerfulness is a gift that we give to others and to ourselves. And, as believers who have been saved by a risen Christ, why shouldn't we be cheerful? The answer, of course, is that we have every reason to honor our Savior with joy in our hearts, smiles on our faces, and words of celebration on our lips.

How cheerful are you? Do you spend most of your day celebrating your life or complaining about it? If you're a big-time celebrator, keep celebrating. But if you've established the bad habit of looking at the hole instead of the donut, it's time to correct your spiritual vision.

Pessimism and doubt are two of the most important tools that the devil uses to achieve his objectives. Your challenge, of course, is to ensure that Satan cannot use these tools on you. So today, make sure to celebrate the life that God has given you. Your Creator has blessed you beyond measure. Honor Him with your prayers, your words, your deeds, and your joy.

It is not fitting, when one is in God's service, to have a gloomy face or a chilling look.

St. Francis of Assisi

Do everything readily and cheerfully—no bickering, no second-guessing allowed! Go out into the world uncorrupted, a breath of fresh air in this squalid and polluted society. Provide people with a glimpse of good living and of the living God. Carry the light-giving Message into the night.

Philippians 2:14-15 MSG

PRIORITIES FOR MY LIFE

Do you need a little cheering up? If so, find somebody else who needs cheering up, too. Then, do your best to brighten that person's day. When you do, you'll discover that cheering up other people is a wonderful way to cheer yourself up, too!

TIMELESS WISDOM FOR GODLY LIVING

God is good, and heaven is forever. And if those two facts don't cheer you up, nothing will.

Marie T. Freeman

Sour godliness is the devil's religion.

John Wesley

We may run, walk, stumble, drive, or fly, but let us never lose sight of the reason for the journey, or miss a chance to see a rainbow on the way.

Gloria Gaither

Hope is the power of being cheerful in circumstances which we know to be desperate.

G. K. Chesterton

> *A happy heart is like a continual feast.*
> Proverbs 15:15 NCV

When I think of God, my heart is so full of joy that the notes leap and dance as they leave my pen; and since God has given me a cheerful heart, I serve him with a cheerful spirit.

Franz Joseph Haydn

A merry heart does good, like medicine.

Proverbs 17:22 NKJV

God loves a cheerful giver.

2 Corinthians 9:7 NIV

A cheerful look brings joy to the heart, and good news gives health to the bones.

Proverbs 15:30 NIV

Is anyone happy? Let him sing songs of praise.

James 5:13 NIV

My Priorities for Life

I do my best to maintain a positive attitude and a cheerful disposition, even when I'm tired or frustrated, or both.

I focus my thoughts on opportunities, not problems.

I consider this day—and every day—to be a gift from God and a cause for celebration.

Check Your Priority		
High	Med.	Low
—	—	—
—	—	—
—	—	—

A Humble Heart

Clothe yourselves with humility toward one another,
because God resists the proud, but gives grace to the humble.

1 Peter 5:5 Holman CSB

We have heard the phrases on countless occasions: "He's a self-made man," or "she's a self-made woman." In truth, none of us are self-made. We all owe countless debts that we can never repay.

Our first debt, of course, is to our Father in heaven—Who has given us everything—and to His Son, Who sacrificed His own life so that we might live eternally. We are also indebted to ancestors, parents, teachers, friends, spouses, family members, coworkers, fellow believers . . . and the list, of course, goes on.

As Christians, we have a profound reason to be humble: We have been refashioned and saved by Jesus Christ, and that salvation came not because of our own good works but because of God's grace. Thus, we are not "self-made," we are "God-made," and "Christ-saved." How, then, can we be boastful? The answer, of course, is that, if we are honest with ourselves and with our God, we simply can't be boastful . . . we must, instead, be eternally grateful and exceedingly humble.

Humility is not, in most cases, a naturally-occurring human trait. Most of us, it seems, are more than willing to stick out our chests and say, "Look at me; I did that!" But in our better moments, in the quiet moments when we search the depths of our own hearts, we know better. Whatever "it" is, God did that, not us. And He deserves the credit.

If you know who you are in Christ, your personal ego is not an issue.

Beth Moore

PRIORITIES FOR MY LIFE

Do you value humility above status? If so, God will smile upon your endeavors. But if you value status above humility, you're inviting God's displeasure. In short, humility pleases God; pride does not.

TIMELESS WISDOM FOR GODLY LIVING

Jesus had a humble heart. If He abides in us, pride will never dominate our lives.

Billy Graham

The humble person will not be thinking humility: He will not be thinking about himself at all.

C. S. Lewis

We see how Jesus clearly chooses the way of humility. He does not appear with great fanfare as a powerful Savior, announcing a new order. On the contrary, he comes quietly, with the many sinners who are receiving a baptism of repentance.

Henri Nouwen

Humble yourselves therefore under the mighty hand of God, so that He may exalt you in due time, casting all your care upon Him, because He cares about you.

1 Peter 5:6-7 Holman CSB

Meekness does not mean being without emotion; it means being in charge of emotion and channeling it in the right direction for the right purpose.

Joyce Meyer

MORE WORDS FROM GOD'S WORD

But He said to me, "My grace is sufficient for you, for power is perfected in weakness." Therefore, I will most gladly boast all the more about my weaknesses, so that Christ's power may reside in me.

2 Corinthians 12:9 Holman CSB

You will save the humble people; But Your eyes are on the haughty, that You may bring them down.

2 Samuel 22:28 NKJV

If My people who are called by My name will humble themselves, and pray and seek My face, and turn from their wicked ways, then I will hear from heaven, and will forgive their sin and heal their land.

2 Chronicles 7:14 NKJV

My Priorities for Life

	Check Your Priority	
High	Med.	Low

I genuinely seek to give God the honor that He deserves.

— — —

I place a high priority on the need to remain humble before God.

— — —

I understand the importance of remaining humble in my dealings with others.

— — —

Aim High

*Live full lives, full in the fullness of God. God can do anything,
you know—far more than you could ever imagine or guess or request in
your wildest dreams! He does it not by pushing us around but
by working within us, his Spirit deeply and gently within us.*

Ephesians 3:19-20 MSG

How big are you willing to dream? Are you willing to entertain the possibility that God has big plans in store for you? Or are you convinced that your future is so dim that you'd better wear night goggles? Well here are the facts, Jack: if you're a believer in the One from Galilee, you have an incredibly bright future ahead of you . . . here on earth and in heaven. That's why you have every right to dream big.

Concentration camp survivor Corrie ten Boom observed, "Every experience God gives us, every person He brings into our lives, is the perfect preparation for the future that only He can see." These words apply to you.

Are you excited about the opportunities of today and thrilled by the possibilities of tomorrow? Do you confidently expect God to lead you to a place of abundance, peace, and joy? And, when your days on earth are over, do you expect to receive the priceless gift of eternal life? If you trust God's promises, and if you have welcomed God's Son into your heart, then you believe that your future is intensely and eternally bright.

It takes courage to dream big dreams. You will discover that courage when you do three things: accept the past, trust God to handle the future, and make the most of the time He has given you today.

Nothing is too difficult for God, and no dreams are too big for Him—not even yours. So start living—and dreaming—accordingly.

The future lies all before us. Shall it only be a slight advance upon what we usually do? Ought it not to be a bound, a leap forward to altitudes of endeavor and success undreamed of before?

Annie Armstrong

When dreams come true, there is life and joy.

Proverbs 13:12 NLT

PRIORITIES FOR MY LIFE

Making your dreams come true requires work. John Maxwell writes "The gap between your vision and your present reality can only be filled through a commitment to maximize your potential." Enough said.

TIMELESS WISDOM FOR GODLY LIVING

To make your dream come true, you have to stay awake.

Dennis Swanberg

Dreaming the dream of God is not for cowards.

Joey Johnson

You cannot out-dream God.

John Eldredge

We must be willing to give up every dream but God's dream.

Larry Crabb

*I came so they can have real and eternal life,
more and better life than they ever dreamed of.*
John 10:10 MSG

You pay God a compliment by asking great things of Him.

St. Teresa of Avila

MORE WORDS FROM GOD'S WORD

It is pleasant to see dreams come true, but fools will not turn from evil to attain them.

Proverbs 13:19 NLT

Be of good courage, and he shall strengthen your heart, all ye that hope in the LORD.

Psalm 31:24 KJV

"I say this because I know what I am planning for you," says the Lord. "I have good plans for you, not plans to hurt you. I will give you hope and a good future."

Jeremiah 29:11 NCV

My Priorities for Life

I try not to place limitations on myself, and I refuse to place limitations on God's power to use me for His purposes.

I prayerfully seek to understand God's plans for my life.

I work to know God's plan for my life, and I work to fulfill that plan.

Check Your Priority		
High	Med.	Low
—	—	—
—	—	—
—	—	—

Above and Beyond Anger

> A *patient person [shows] great understanding,*
> *but a quick-tempered one promotes foolishness.*
>
> Proverbs 14:29 Holman CSB

I f you're like most people, you know a thing or two about anger. After all, everybody gets mad occasionally, and you're no exception.

Anger is a natural human emotion that is sometimes necessary and appropriate. Even Jesus became angry when confronted with the moneychangers in the temple: "And Jesus entered the temple and drove out all those who were buying and selling in the temple, and overturned the tables of the moneychangers and the seats of those who were selling doves" (Matthew 21:12 NASB).

Righteous indignation is an appropriate response to evil, but God does not intend that anger should rule our lives. Far from it. God intends that we turn away from anger whenever possible and forgive our neighbors just as we seek forgiveness for ourselves.

Life is full of frustrations: some great and some small. On occasion, you, like Jesus, will confront evil, and when you do, you may respond as He did: vigorously and without reservation. But, more often your frustrations will be of the more mundane variety. As long as you live here on earth, you will face countless opportunities to lose your temper over small, relatively insignificant events: a traffic jam, an inconsiderate comment, or a broken promise. When you are tempted to lose your temper over the minor inconveniences of life, don't. Instead of turning up the heat, walk away. Turn away from anger, hatred, bitterness, and regret. Turn, instead, to God. When you do, you'll be following His commandments and giving yourself a priceless gift . . . the gift of peace.

Acrid bitterness inevitably seeps into the lives of people who harbor grudges and suppress anger, and bitterness is always a poison.

Lee Strobel

PRIORITIES FOR MY LIFE

Time Out!: If you become angry, the time to step away from the situation is before you say unkind words or do unkind things— not after. It's perfectly okay to place yourself in "time out" until you can calm down.

Anger is the noise of the soul; the unseen irritant of the heart; the relentless invader of silence.

Max Lucado

Anger unresolved will only bring you woe.

Kay Arthur

When you strike out in anger, you may miss the other person, but you will always hit yourself.

Jim Gallery

Anger breeds remorse in the heart, discord in the home, bitterness in the community, and confusion in the state.

Billy Graham

But now you must also put away all the following:
anger, wrath, malice, slander,
and filthy language from your mouth.
Colossians 3:8 Holman CSB

Life is too short to spend it being angry, bored, or dull.

Barbara Johnson

Don't let your spirit rush to be angry, for anger abides in the heart of fools.

Ecclesiastes 7:9 Holman CSB

All bitterness, anger and wrath, insult and slander must be removed from you, along with all wickedness. And be kind and compassionate to one another, forgiving one another, just as God also forgave you in Christ.

Ephesians 4:31-32 Holman CSB

Everyone must be quick to hear, slow to speak, and slow to anger, for man's anger does not accomplish God's righteousness.

James 1:19-20 Holman CSB

But I tell you that men will have to give account on the day of judgment for every careless word they have spoken. For by your words you will be acquitted, and by your words you will be condemned.

Matthew 12:36-37 NIV

My Priorities for Life

	Check Your Priority	
High	Med.	Low

When I forgive others, I feel better about myself.

— — —

I understand the need to accept my past and forgive those who have hurt me.

— — —

I understand the importance of controlling my temper.

— — —

The Joys of a Clear Conscience

So I strive always to keep my conscience clear before God and man.

Acts 24:16 NIV

It has been said that character is what we are when nobody is watching. How true. When we do things that we know aren't right, we try to hide them from our families and friends. But even then, God is watching.

Few things in life torment us more than a guilty conscience. And, few things in life provide more contentment than the knowledge that we are obeying God's commandments. A clear conscience is one of the rewards we earn when we obey God's Word and follow His will. When we follow God's will and accept His gift of salvation, our earthly rewards are never-ceasing, and our heavenly rewards are everlasting.

Do you place a high value on the need to keep your conscience clear? If so, keep up the good work. But if you're tempted to do something that you'd rather the world not know about, remember this: You can sometimes keep secrets from other people, but you can never keep secrets from God. God knows what you think and what you do. And if you want to please Him, you must start with good intentions, a pure heart, and a clear conscience.

If you sincerely wish to honor your Father in heaven, follow His commandments. When you do, your character will take care of itself . . . and so will your conscience. Then, as you journey through life, you won't need to look over your shoulder to see who—besides God—is watching.

God desires that we become spiritually healthy enough through faith to have a conscience that rightly interprets the work of the Holy Spirit.

Beth Moore

Do not conform any longer to the pattern of this world,
but be transformed by the renewing of your mind.
Then you will be able to test and approve what God's will is—his good,
pleasing and perfect will.

Romans 12:2 NIV

PRIORITIES FOR MY LIFE

The more important the decision . . . the more carefully you should listen to your conscience.

TIMELESS WISDOM FOR GODLY LIVING

Every secret act of character, conviction, and courage has been observed in living color by our omniscient God.

Bill Hybels

Your conscience is your alarm system. It's your protection.

Charles Stanley

The voice of the subconscious argues with you, tries to convince you; but the inner voice of God does not argue; it does not try to convince you. It just speaks, and it is self-authenticating.

E. Stanley Jones

The convicting work of the Holy Spirit awakens, disturbs, and judges.

Franklin Graham

Let us draw near to God with a sincere heart in full assurance of faith, having our hearts sprinkled to cleanse us from a guilty conscience and having our bodies washed with pure water.

Hebrews 10:22 NIV

He that loses his conscience has nothing left that is worth keeping.

Izaak Walton

MORE WORDS FROM GOD'S WORD

I will maintain my righteousness and never let go of it; my conscience will not reproach me as long as I live.

Job 27:6 NIV

Create in me a pure heart, O God, and renew a steadfast spirit within me.

Psalm 51:10 NIV

For indeed, the kingdom of God is within you.

Luke 17:21 NKJV

If then you were raised with Christ, seek those things which are above, where Christ is, sitting at the right hand of God. Set your mind on things above, not on things on the earth.

Colossians 3:1-2 NKJV

My Priorities for Life

I believe that it is important that I attune my thoughts to God's will for my life.

I understand the value of a clear conscience.

When I prepare to make an important decision, I listen to my conscience very carefully.

Check Your Priority		
High	Med.	Low
—	—	—
—	—	—
—	—	—

God's Surprising Plans

Who are those who fear the Lord? He will show them the path
they should choose. They will live in prosperity,
and their children will inherit the Promised Land.

Psalm 25:12-13 NLT

The Bible makes it clear: God's got a plan—a whopper of a plan—and you play a vitally important role in it. But here's the catch: God won't force His plans upon you; you've got to figure things out for yourself . . . or not.

As a Christian, you should ask yourself this question: "How closely can I make my plans match God's plans?" The more closely you manage to follow the path that God intends for your life, the better.

Do you have questions or concerns about the future? Take them to God in prayer. Do you have hopes and expectations? Talk to God about your dreams. Are you carefully planning for the days and weeks ahead? Consult God as you establish your priorities. Turn every concern over to your Heavenly Father, and sincerely seek His guidance—prayerfully, earnestly, and often. Then, listen for His answers . . . and trust the answers that He gives.

Sometimes, God's plans are crystal clear, but other times, He may lead you through the wilderness before He delivers you to the Promised Land. So be patient, keep praying, and keep seeking His will for your life. When you do, you will be amazed at the marvelous things that an all-powerful, all-knowing God can do.

Simplicity, clarity, singleness: These are the attributes that give our lives power and vividness and joy as they are also the marks of great art. They seem to be the purpose of God for his whole creation.

Richard Holloway

PRIORITIES FOR MY LIFE

Waiting faithfully for God's plan to unfold is more important than understanding God's plan. Ruth Bell Graham once said, "When I am dealing with an all-powerful, all-knowing God, I, as a mere mortal, must offer my petitions not only with persistence, but also with patience. Someday I'll know why." Even when you can't understand God's plans, you must trust Him and never lose faith!

God will not permit any troubles to come upon us unless He has a specific plan by which great blessing can come out of the difficulty.

Peter Marshall

In God's plan, God is the standard for perfection. We don't compare ourselves to others; they are just as fouled up as we are. The goal is to be like him; anything less is inadequate.

Max Lucado

God in Christ is the author and finisher of my faith. He knows exactly what needs to happen in my life for my faith to grow. He designs the perfect program for me.

Mary Morrison Suggs

> *And we know that in all things God works for the good of those who love him, who have been called according to his purpose.*
> *Romans 8:28 NIV*

God has His reasons. He has His purposes. Ours is an intentional God, brimming over with motive and mission. He never does things capriciously or decides with the flip of a coin.

Joni Eareckson Tada

The steps of the Godly are directed by the Lord. He delights in every detail of their lives. Though they stumble, they will not fall, for the Lord holds them by the hand.

Psalm 37:23-24 NLT

"For I know the plans I have for you," declares the Lord, "plans to prosper you and not to harm you, plans to give you hope and a future. Then you will call upon me and come and pray to me, and I will listen to you."

Jeremiah 29:11-12 NIV

The Lord says, "I will guide you along the best pathway for your life. I will advise you and watch over you."

Psalm 32:8 NLT

My Priorities for Life

Since I believe that God has a plan for my day, I set aside quiet time each morning in order to seek His will for my life.

Since God created me, I will trust Him to know what's best for me.

Since I trust that God's plans have eternal ramifications, I will seek His will for my life.

Check Your Priority		
High	Med.	Low
—	—	—
—	—	—
—	—	—

This
Is the Day . . .

This is the day which the LORD has made;
let us rejoice and be glad in it.

Psalm 118:24 NASB

The familiar words of Psalm 118 remind us that today, like every day, is a priceless gift from God. What do you expect from the day ahead? Are you expecting God to do wonderful things, or are you living beneath a cloud of apprehension and doubt? Do you expect God to use you in unexpected ways, or do you expect another uneventful day to pass with little fanfare? As a thoughtful believer, the answer to these questions should be obvious.

C. H. Spurgeon, the renowned 19th-century English clergymen, advised, "Rejoicing is clearly a spiritual command. To ignore it, I need to remind you, is disobedience." As Christians, we are called by our Creator to live abundantly, prayerfully, and joyfully. To do otherwise is to squander His spiritual gifts.

If you're a thoughtful Christian, then you're a thankful Christian. And because of your faith, you can face the inevitable challenges and disappointments of each day armed with the joy of Christ and the promise of salvation.

So whatever this day holds for you, begin it and end it with God as your partner and Christ as your Savior. And throughout the day, give thanks to the One who created you and saved you. God's love for you is infinite—accept it joyfully and be thankful.

Live today fully, expressing gratitude
for all you have been,
all you are right now,
and all you are becoming.

Melodie Beattie

PRIORITIES FOR MY LIFE

Today, like every other day, provides countless opportunities to serve God and to worship Him. But, if we turn our backs on our Creator, or if we simply become too busy to acknowledge His greatness, we do a profound disservice to ourselves, to our families, and to our world.

TIMELESS WISDOM FOR GODLY LIVING

Today is a gift from God. That's why it is called "The Present."

Anonymous

Every day of our lives we make choices about how we're going to live that day.

Luci Swindoll

Wherever you are, be all there. Live to the hilt every situation you believe to be the will of God.

Jim Elliot

Today is mine. Tomorrow is none of my business. If I peer anxiously into the fog of the future, I will strain my spiritual eyes so that I will not see clearly what is required of me now.

Elisabeth Elliot

For he says, "In the time of my favor I heard you, and in the day of salvation I helped you." I tell you, now is the time of God's favor, now is the day of salvation.
2 Corinthians 6:2 NIV

With each new dawn, life delivers a package to your front door, rings your doorbell, and runs.

Charles Swindoll

Encourage one another daily, as long as it is Today . . . .

Hebrews 3:13 NIV

Give your entire attention to what God is doing right now, and don't get worked up about what may or may not happen tomorrow. God will help you deal with whatever hard things come up when the time comes.

Matthew 6:34 MSG

For he says, "In the time of my favor I heard you, and in the day of salvation I helped you." I tell you, now is the time of God's favor, now is the day of salvation.

2 Corinthians 6:2 NIV

Rejoice in the Lord always. I will say it again: Rejoice!

Philippians 4:4 Holman CSB

My Priorities for Life

I believe that it is important to live passionately, obediently, and joyfully.

I trust that the way I choose to live today will have a profound impact on my future.

I understand that today is a precious gift.

	Check Your Priority	
High	Med.	Low
—	—	—
—	—	—
—	—	—

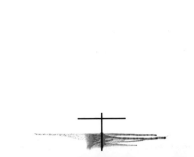

*The thing you should want most is
God's kingdom and doing what God wants.
Then all these other things you need
will be given to you.*

Matthew 6:33 NCV

TOPIC	TITLE	PAGE

God's Priorities for Your Life for Teens